WINE DOGS
California

"Yesterday, I was a dog. Today, I am a dog.
Tomorrow, I will probably be a dog.
There's just so little hope of advancement."

SNOOPY

WINE DOGS
California

A PICTORIAL CELEBRATION OF CANINES
FROM THE GREAT WINE ESTATES OF CALIFORNIA

BY CRAIG McGILL AND SUSAN ELLIOTT

GIANT DOG

 RUBY SEVEN-YEAR-OLD QUEENSLAND RED HEELER, BRIDLEWOOD ESTATE WINERY, SANTA YNEZ CA

CONTENTS

BETTY-JANE

PET PEEVE: FLYING BUGS
FAVORITE FOOD: CHICKEN
OWNERS: ROBERT AND PAT PARKER
FAVORITE TOY: ANYTHING STUFFED AND SQUEAKY
OBSESSIONS: KICKING HER HIND LEGS AND DANCING
NAUGHTIEST DEED: DOING DOO-DOOS IN THE LIVING ROOM
FAVORITE PASTIME: SLEEPING WITH BUDDY, HER BEST FRIEND

BUDDY

OBSESSION: PILLOWS
PET PEEVE: BUBBLEWRAP
OWNERS: ROBERT AND PAT PARKER
NAUGHTIEST DEED: DOING DOO-DOOS IN THE PET-SITTER'S ROOM FOR SPITE
FAVORITE PASTIME: BITING AT RAINDROPS
FAVORITE FOODS: CONFIT AND LIVERWURST
FAVORITE TOY: ANYTHING THAT BETTY-JANE CAN PULL AWAY

FOREWORD

by Robert M. Parker Jr

I AM HONORED and pleased to write this introduction about wine dogs in California. In short, I believe dogs are one of God's greatest gifts to mankind. I have had dogs since I was born, and they have been an unending source of joy, pleasure, and companionship. Throughout my childhood and teenage years, our dogs were cocker spaniels, which my mother adored and treated like spoiled children. In all of my childhood memories, I recall them always at my side. My father, who was a serious hunter, also kept a pack of hound dogs, mostly blue tick hounds and ones he called red bone, as their hair, not bones, was red. Unlike the cocker spaniels, they were kept outside, but they were a great source of rough-housing and play. As an only child in a rural environment, they provided me with immense joy and companionship, and often served as the sibling pals I lacked while growing up.

Going away to college and law school meant no live-in pets, but it was always fun to return home where the dogs greeted me as if I were their favorite person in the world. After we were married, my wife and I acquired a dog I had always wanted to have, a three-month-old basset hound named Watson. Something about their long, droopy ears, half-opened, bloodshot eyes, lethargic personalities, and expressive song (their whining and howling) has always appealed to me. Since 1969, we have had a succession of basset hounds in our lives, every one of them completely different in personality, but all sharing the breed's love of eating, sniffing, and chasing ... anything ... their owners, tennis balls, or some of the feral cats in the area.

Fifteen years ago we added an extraordinary English bulldog named George, another breed we had always wanted to own because we thought they looked like little old men or canine versions of a Buddha. George became quite a celebrity as he was featured in many of the profiles written on me. An incredibly photogenic chap, he had two large black patches around his broad-set eyes, making visitors often call him "The Lone Ranger" or the "Masked Man." George won the top performance by a canine in a documentary movie at the Cannes Film Festival in 2004. Instead of the Palme d'Or, which is given to the year's top movie, he won the "Palme Dog." On the day he passed away at age 12, I tried to give him CPR, but he died instantly, which spared us the pain of having to have him euthanized. His successor, Buddy (named after my father), is almost an identical clone – relentless in his play, and obsessed with bumblebees or anything that makes him run around like a crazy man.

Of course, dogs are also an intricate part of vineyards. One of the most famous stories about my career involves a nasty schnauzer at Château Cheval Blanc in Bordeaux's famed Saint-Émilion region. In 1983, while visiting Bordeaux and tasting the 1982 vintage, Cheval Blanc's owner, Jacques Hébrard, refused to let me taste his wine. One evening I called him and presented my arguments on why I should be permitted to taste. He told me to come on over, which I did. After knocking on the door, I was greeted by an eight-to ten-pound schnauzer who quickly attached his teeth to my ankle. Mr Hébrard didn't bat an eye, and after what seemed like a long period of time, the schnauzer let go, but not before ripping my pants and socks and tearing my skin. As I sat at a desk listening to Mr Hébrard berate me for not understanding his wines, not one word was mentioned about the schnauzer's sneak attack or, for that matter, my bloody ankle. I always thought that if I were to ever commit a crime against a dog (a cardinal sin the way I see it), it would be against that dog. However, he passed away several years later, and the story became embellished and exaggerated in wine circles both abroad and here in the States, with several French stories suggesting I was behind the dog's demise.

After twenty-eight years in this profession, it is wonderful to see how many times winery dogs are sitting at the top of a ridge line, watching their owners direct a vineyard's harvest, or sleeping next to the fermenter or beside their master's desk.

BORED. BORED. BORED. I'M STARVING.

WHERE ARE THEY? THEY NEVER FEED ME.

WAIT... WAS THAT THE REFRIGERATOR?

THOUGHT I SMELT LIVERWURST... MMMM

IT'S MY FAVORITE.

OUTTA MY WAY BETTY-JANE...

I have always admonished friends that anyone who did not love a dog had to be approached with considerable suspicion, and would probably not be someone with whom I would want to spend much time. Dogs are indeed a special gift to all of us. They give us companionship, they act as full-time therapists, they amuse us, and they lift our spirits when we're down.

It is often said that a vine is most content in the shadow of a man. If that is true, then a dog is also happiest when it is in the shadow of its owner.

I love the previous books that Craig and Sue have put together, and hope this edition of *Wine Dogs California* is a howling success ... as my bulldog Buddy would say.

ROBERT M. PARKER JR WAS BORN IN BALTIMORE, MARYLAND AND INITIALLY PURSUED A CAREER IN LAW. HIS INTEREST IN WINE BEGAN IN 1967 AND IT WASN'T LONG BEFORE ROBERT HAD STARTED TO CARVE OUT A SPECTACULAR CAREER IN WINE WRITING THAT NOW SPANS OVER 28 YEARS. HE IS THE FOUNDER OF *THE WINE ADVOCATE* AND IS THE CONTRIBUTING EDITOR FOR *FOOD AND WINE* MAGAZINE. HE ALSO PERIODICALLY CONTRIBUTES TO OTHER MAGAZINES INCLUDING *THE FIELD* AND FRANCE'S *L'EXPRESS*. HE IS THE AUTHOR OF MANY BEST-SELLING AND AWARDED WINE BOOKS INCLUDING *BORDEAUX, BURGUNDY, PARKER'S WINE BUYER'S GUIDE* AND *THE WINES OF THE RHÔNE VALLEY AND PROVENCE*. ROBERT'S BULLDOG GEORGE WON THE COVETED 'PALME DOG' PRIZE AT THE CANNES FILM FESTIVAL FOR BEST CANINE PERFORMANCE IN A FILM FOR HIS CAMEO IN THE DOCUMENTARY *MONDOVINO*. WWW.EROBERTPARKER.COM
THIS STORY HAS BEEN ADAPTED AND REPRINTED FROM *WINE DOGS USA*, PUBLISHED 2006.

ABBY

FAVORITE FOOD: LASAGNE
OBSESSION: HANK'S BALLS
FAVORITE TOY: PINK MONKEY
FAVORITE PASTIME: SWIMMING
OWNERS: KAREN AND GIO GRANDINETTI
PET PEEVE: STAYING UP PAST HER BEDTIME
NAUGHTIEST DEED: STEALING AN ENTIRE PAN OF LASAGNE

HANK

FAVORITE TOY: SHEEPIE
OBSESSION: BALLS BALLS BALLS
FAVORITE PASTIME: FLOATING THE RIVER
OWNERS: RUSSELL FROM AND VAILIA ESH
FAVORITE FOODS: MIXED NUTS AND MEAT PIES
NAUGHTIEST DEED: SOME MATERIAL IS NOT FIT FOR CHILDREN

RIVA

PET PEEVE: BATHS
FAVORITE TOY: OTTO
NAUGHTIEST DEED: SAMPLING LOW-HANGING FRUIT FROM THE VINES
OWNERS: ELLEN AND GARY LUCHTEL
OBSESSION: WHATEVER YOU'RE DOING
FAVORITE PASTIME: RIDING AROUND IN THE GOLF CART

OTTO

PET PEEVE: BEING TOLD TO DO ANYTHING HE DOESN'T WANT TO DO
OWNERS: ELLEN AND GARY LUCHTEL
FAVORITE FOODS: RIVA'S LEFTOVERS AND THE NEIGHBOR'S CAT FOOD
OBSESSION: CHECKING ON FRUIT STATUS
NAUGHTIEST DEED: CHASING (AND CATCHING) RABBITS

HALEY

OWNERS: ELLEN AND GARY LUCHTEL
KNOWN ACCOMPLICES: OTTO AND RIVA
FAVORITE FOOD: OLD AMSTERDAM GOUDA
OBSESSION: DOING HER BEST TO BE THE CENTER OF ATTENTION
NAUGHTIEST DEED: CHEWING THROUGH UNOPENED WINE BOXES
FAVORITE PASTIME: CHASING PRETTY MUCH ANYTHING THAT MOVES
PET PEEVE: HAVING TO BE INDOORS WHEN FRIENDS ARE ENJOYING THE WEATHER

DIZZY

OBSESSION: SLEEP
FAVORITE TOY: STEVE
OWNER: STEVE ALLEN
FAVORITE FOOD: ALL FOOD
PET PEEVE: BEING LEFT HOME
NAUGHTIEST DEED: STEALING FOOD
FAVORITE PASTIME: WATCHING CHLOE RUN AROUND

TIGER WINSTON

FAVORITE FOOD: POPCORN
OBSESSION: HIS NEXT MEAL
OWNERS: GARY AND ROSELLA FRANSCIONI
NAUGHTIEST DEED: IGNORING GARY AND ROSELLA WHEN HE SEES THEM WITH SUITCASES
PET PEEVE: BEING LEFT ALONE, EVEN FOR AN HOUR
FAVORITE TOY: EACH AND EVERY ONE OF HIS STUFFED TOYS
FAVORITE PASTIME: BEING CO-PILOT IN THE TRUCK WITH GARY

BONES

OWNER: ASHLEY KEEVER
FAVORITE FOOD: BURRITOS
PET PEEVE: BEING LEFT OUT
NAUGHTIEST DEED: HELPING HIMSELF TO WHATEVER'S ON YOUR PLATE
OBSESSION: WAITING FOR THINGS TO CHASE
FAVORITE PASTIME: CHASING RABBITS, DEER AND TURKEY VULTURES THROUGH THE VINEYARD
KNOWN ACCOMPLICE: LILIANA, HIS BABY SISTER

CHLOE

OWNER: NILS VENGE
OBSESSION: FISHING IN THE CREEK
PET PEEVE: NOT GETTING ENOUGH PLAYTIME IN THE VINEYARD
FAVORITE FOOD: CABERNET GRAPES
NAUGHTIEST DEED: FISHING IN THE CREEK
FAVORITE PASTIME: RETRIEVING A SQUEAKY BALL

SADIE

FAVORITE FOOD: COLD CUTS
OBSESSION: GREETING VISITORS
OWNERS: JOHN AND FELICIA TUDAL
FAVORITE TOY: PABLO, THE RANCH FOREMAN
PET PEEVE: NOT SPENDING ENOUGH TIME WITH THE BOYS, COOPER AND TUCKER, FROM SHIBUMI KNOLL
FAVORITE PASTIMES: RACING ALONGSIDE VINEYARD TRACTORS AND OVERSEEING PRODUCTION OF 'SADIE'S CUVEE'
NAUGHTIEST DEEDS: EATING THE CAT FOOD AND CHASING CHICKENS

JOEY

FAVORITE FOOD: WAFFLES
OBSESSION: PLAYING FETCH
OWNERS: TIM AND MARY LOUISE BUCHER
NAUGHTIEST DEED: COUNTER SURFING TO STEAL A BAG OF ROLLS AND A PLATE OF CHICKEN
PET PEEVE: ANY STUFFED DOG CUTER THAN HE IS
FAVORITE PASTIME: BEING MARY LOUISE'S SHADOW

CHELSEA

NAUGHTIEST DEED: 'SHEARING' MARY LOUISE'S SHEEPSKIN SLIPPERS
OWNERS: TIM AND MARY LOUISE BUCHER
FAVORITE FOOD: PIECES OF PUMPKIN CARVED FROM A HALLOWEEN JACK-O-LANTERN
FAVORITE PASTIME: ESCAPING AND WANDERING FOR HOURS UNTIL HER STOMACH TELLS HER IT IS TIME TO COME HOME

SNICKERS

PET PEEVE: PUPPIES
FAVORITE TOY: KONG
FAVORITE FOOD: TREATS
OBSESSION: SUNBATHING
OWNER: JAY WILDEROTTER
FAVORITE PASTIME: BEING THE OFFICIAL TASTING ROOM GREETER
NAUGHTIEST DEED: TEARING UP DOG BEDS

PHOENIX

PET PEEVE: FIREWORKS
FAVORITE TOY: SQUEAKY TENNIS BALLS
FAVORITE PASTIME: CHASING RABBITS
OWNERS: ROSY AND CHRIS WILDEROTTER
FAVORITE FOOD: ANYTHING BUT DRY KIBBLE
OBSESSIONS: SQUIRRELS, RABBITS AND SQUEAKERS
NAUGHTIEST DEED: DE-STUFFING TOYS IN TEN SECONDS FLAT

YOGI

OBSESSION: CHEWING
FAVORITE TOY: RAWHIDES
PET PEEVE: BEING LEFT ALONE
OWNERS: ROSY AND CHRIS WILDEROTTER
NAUGHTIEST DEED: DESTROYING THE YARD
FAVORITE PASTIME: WRESTLING WITH PHOENIX

AUSTRALIAN SHEPHERD X, 9 & LABRADOR, 1 | **WILDEROTTER VINEYARD** PLYMOUTH, CA

SOPHIA

FAVORITE FOOD: MEAT
FAVORITE TOY: TENNIS BALL
OBSESSIONS: CATS AND RABBITS
OWNERS: BROOKE AND ERNST STORM
PET PEEVE: BEING LEFT ALONE FOR TOO LONG
NAUGHTIEST DEED: PUSHING THE TRASH CAN OVER AND SPREADING IT ALL OVER THE HOUSE
FAVORITE PASTIME: DRIVING AROUND WITH ERNST

DUTCHESS

OWNER: DEBRA MATHY
FAVORITE FOOD: BULA STICK
KNOWN ACCOMPLICE: AMMIE
NAUGHTIEST DEED: SITTING DOWN IN THE VINEYARD DURING HER WALK
FAVORITE PASTIMES: HANGING WITH DEBRA AND SWIMMING IN THE CREEK
OBSESSION: CHASING THE LASER DOT
PET PEEVE: BEING LEFT WITH A BABYSITTER
FAVORITE TOYS: HER SCHOOL LEARNING TOYS

LABRADOR, 7 | **DUTCHER CROSSING WINERY** GEYSERVILLE, CA

SOONIE

PET PEEVE: BEING MOVED WHILE SLEEPING ON A FAMILY MEMBER'S PILLOW
OWNERS: MANON AND JULIETTE MURPHY
OBSESSION: STUFFED ANIMALS TO FIGHT WITH
FAVORITE PASTIME: CHASING IMAGINARY BIRDS
NAUGHTIEST DEED: TAKING ADVANTAGE OF DISTRACTED FAMILY MEMBERS SO SHE CAN STEAL FOOD
KNOWN ACCOMPLICE: HER BEST FRIEND, TRUFFLE THE CAT

POSIP

PET PEEVE: CATS
FAVORITE TOY: A BALL
NAUGHTIEST DEED: JUMPING UP TO KISS PEOPLE AND DIRTYING THEIR SHIRTS
OWNER: MILJENKO GRGICH (MIKE), PICTURED
FAVORITE PASTIMES: PLAYING WITH BOCCE BALLS, CHASING SQUIRRELS, TURKEYS AND OTHER BIRDS

BORDER COLLIE X, 7 | **GRGICH HILLS ESTATE** RUTHERFORD, CA

BEAN

FAVORITE TOY: STICKS
PET PEEVE: CLOSED DOORS
OWNER: MELISSA STADLER
OBSESSIONS: FOOD AND STICKS
FAVORITE PASTIMES: BEGGING AND FETCHING
NAUGHTIEST DEED: TAKING CRACKERS FROM THE HANDS OF UNSUSPECTING TASTING ROOM GUESTS

ZUCCHINI

FAVORITE FOOD: ROAST CHICKEN
OWNER: STEPHANIE SIMUNOVICH
OBSESSION: CHASING ANYTHING THAT'S THROWN
FAVORITE TOY: THE NEXT ONE HE GETS TO DESTROY
NAUGHTIEST DEED: CHEWING STEPHANIE'S THINGS WHEN THEY ARE LEFT ON THE COFFEE TABLE
PET PEEVE: NOT GETTING INVITED INTO THE BED TO SLEEP

TULE BOLLIBAKKA

OWNERS: KATHLEEN AND SCOTT McLEOD
FAVORITE TOY: SCOTT'S OLD TENNIS SHOE
FAVORITE FOOD: KIBBLE (ALL THAT HE KNOWS)
NAUGHTIEST DEED: CHEWING A COMPUTER CORD
PET PEEVE: OTHER ANIMALS GETTING ATTENTION
OBSESSION: CHEWING, CHEWING AND MORE CHEWING
KNOWN ACCOMPLICES: STRIPEY, BLACKIE, GUINEA AND THE PEACOCK
FAVORITE PASTIME: RUNNING DOWN VINEYARD ROWS TO ROLL IN LEAVES

SILVER OAK CELLARS OAKVILLE, CA | LABRADOR, 11 WEEKS

VIVA LA RIVA

OBSESSION: DAVID
NAUGHTIEST DEED: EATING A PIZZA FROM OFF THE KITCHEN COUNTER
OWNERS: DR. KARY AND DAVID R. DUNCAN
FAVORITE TOY: ANYTHING SHE IS ALLOWED TO CHEW
FAVORITE PASTIMES: CHASING BIRDS AND SLEEPING
FAVORITE FOOD: ANYTHING THAT PAIRS WITH CABERNET

DAISY

FAVORITE TOY: SOCKS
OWNER: SALLY ALLRED
PET PEEVE: GETTING A BATH
NAUGHTIEST DEED: HIDING OUT UNDER BLANKETS
FAVORITE PASTIME: SITTING ON LAPS AND BEING LOVED UP
OBSESSIONS: BACON AND BELLY RUBS

OWNERS: DOUG AND ANNETTE SHAFER
OBSESSION: ROLLING ON THE FRONT LAWN
FAVORITE PASTIMES: RACING THE HALLWAYS OF THE WINERY AND STRIKING NOBLE POSES
PET PEEVE: NOT BEING FED EVERY HALF HOUR
FAVORITE FOOD: DOGGIE TREATS FROM THE KITCHEN
NAUGHTIEST DEED: EATING A SANDWICH OUT OF A VISITOR'S PURSE

CODY

GOLDEN RETRIEVER, 2 | **SHAFER VINEYARDS** NAPA, CA

ALFIE

OWNER: ROSE GALANTY
PET PEEVE: ANKLE BITERS
FAVORITE FOOD: WILD SALMON
NAUGHTIEST DEED: DANCING IN THE STREET
FAVORITE PASTIME: CHANNELING URI GELLER
FAVORITE TOYS: SQUEAKY SQUIRREL AND DUCK

WALLY BOBBY JR.

OWNER: TRACI SEVILLE
FAVORITE FOOD: CAT FOOD
OBSESSION: CHLOË THE CAT
PET PEEVE: HAVING TO GO IN HIS CRATE
NAUGHTIEST DEED: EATING HIS AUNTIE'S FAVORITE SHOES
FAVORITE PASTIME: RIDING ON THE STAND-UP PADDLEBOARD
KNOWN ACCOMPLICES: PEYTON AND RILEY FROM FONTELLA FAMILY WINERY

ROARK

OWNER: TRACI SEVILLE
FAVORITE FOOD: CHEESE
FAVORITE TOY: ORBEE BALL
OBSESSION: THE CAT'S LASER POINTER
NAUGHTIEST DEED: STEALING AN ENTIRE CHEESECAKE FROM THE COUNTER
PET PEEVES: HAVING TO STAY HOME AND WALLY BOBBY JR. YELLING AT HIM

From left: **WINNIE:** *FAVORITE FOOD: SOMETHING UNMENTIONABLE INVOLVING ALBERT THE CAT*
PET PEEVES: BUSTER BOSSING HER AROUND AND EATING HER COLLARS
OWNERS: MARK AND TRACY BURNINGHAM

BUSTER: *OBSESSION: FETCHING THE PAPER IN THE MORNING*
FAVORITE PASTIME: JUMPING IN THE LAKE
OWNER: BARBARA SCHUBEL

BUSTER: *FAVORITE PASTIME: EATING UNDERWEAR, ROCKS AND SISTER WINNIE'S COLLARS*
FAVORITE FOOD: UNDERWEAR
OWNERS: MARK AND TRACY BURNINGHAM

LABRADOR 7 MONTHS LABRADOR

From left: **KAYLEE:** *FAVORITE TOY: NINJA BUNNY*
NAUGHTIEST DEED: TRYING TO HERD THE WINEMAKER
OWNERS: LEILANI, AEDYN AND CHRISTINE CAREY

BLUIE: *FAVORITE FOOD: TOAST*
NAUGHTIEST DEED: TACKLING AND DRAGGING CHARLIE AROUND BY HIS SOCKS
OWNERS: CHRIS AND DAWN BENZIGER

SADIE: *FAVORITE FOOD: THANKSGIVING TURKEY*
FAVORITE PASTIME: CHASING RABBITS AND HORSES
OWNER: AMY COLLINS

FRANKIE: *NAUGHTIEST DEED: GREETING PEOPLE TOO PASSIONATELY*
OBSESSION: BRIGHT YELLOW TENNIS BALLS
OWNER: MICHAEL O'LOONEY

BRADOR, 7 MONTHS, AUSTRALIAN SHEPHERD X, 4, LABRADOR, 8 MONTHS, ST. BERNARD, 4 & GOLDEN RETRIEVER, 3 | **BENZIGER FAMILY WINERY** GLEN ELLEN, CA

SAWYER

OWNER: HUNTER RUSACK
FAVORITE FOOD: STEAK
FAVORITE TOY: GEOFF'S SHOES
FAVORITE PASTIME: LYING DOWN
NAUGHTIEST DEED: LOSING GEOFF'S SHOE
OBSESSION: BARKING AT THE NEIGHBOR'S DOGS
PET PEEVE: GETTING CAUGHT TAKING GEOFF'S SHOE

STAR

OWNER: PARKER RUSACK
FAVORITE PASTIME: ACTING LIKE SHE'S IN CHARGE
FAVORITE TOY: TACO THE CAT
OBSESSION: RAPIDLY BARKING AT ANYONE OR ANYTHING NEW
NAUGHTIEST DEED: ROLLING IN DEAD ANIMALS
PET PEEVE: GETTING PICKED UP BY LITTLE GIRLS

MANDY

OWNER: AUSTIN RUSACK
OBSESSION: COLLECTING THE NEWSPAPER EVERY MORNING
PET PEEVE: BEING LEFT BEHIND
FAVORITE TOY: STUFFED SQUIRREL
NAUGHTIEST DEED: JUMPING INTO (AND GETTING STUCK IN) AN EMPTY DUMPSTER
FAVORITE PASTIME: RUNNING WITH GEOFF

GYPSY

FAVORITE TOY: THE BEAR
FAVORITE PASTIME: SLEEPING
FAVORITE FOOD: TURKEY JERKY
PET PEEVE: PANDORA THE CAT
OWNERS: TOM AND BEVERLY RINALDI
NAUGHTIEST DEED: HUMPING THE BEAR
OBSESSION: WAITING FOR TOM TO COME TO RUB HER BELLY

AMOS

FAVORITE FOOD: ALMONDS
OBSESSION: GIVING HUGS
PET PEEVE: GETTING OUT OF BED
OWNERS: CHELSEA AND AUSTIN HAWLEY
FAVORITE TOYS: BUNGS AND TENNIS BALLS
FAVORITE PASTIMES: CAR RIDES AND BOAT RIDES ON LAKE SONOMA
NAUGHTIEST DEED: EATING A WHOLE PIZZA FROM OFF THE COUNTER

GLADYS

OBSESSION: TREATS!!!
PET PEEVE: ROLLERBLADES
OWNER: KATHARINE TAYLOR
FAVORITE PASTIME: SUNBATHING
FAVORITE FOOD: STEEL-HEAD SALMON
KNOWN ACCOMPLICE: PATSY THE HUNGARIAN VIZSLA
FAVORITE TOY: A TWO-FOOT-TALL STUFFED MINNIE MOUSE
NAUGHTIEST DEED: SAMPLING THE CONTENTS OF GUESTS' PICNIC BASKETS

PUG, 4 | **SAUCELITO CANYON VINEYARD** SAN LUIS OBISPO, CA

REMI

PET PEEVE: PING PONG
OWNER: JON EMMERICH
FAVORITE FOOD: GRAPES ON THE VINE
NAUGHTIEST DEED: LIFTING TOM'S KILT IN THE TASTING ROOM
OBSESSION: WANTING TO MEET AND GREET EVERYONE SHE SEES
FAVORITE TOYS: WINE CORKS AND VINEYARD WORKERS' GLOVES
FAVORITE PASTIME: PLAYING WITH SADIE, GEORGE AND TINY AT ALSTON PARK

SILVERADO VINEYARDS NAPA, CA | GREAT DANE, 2

PRESLEY

FAVORITE FOOD: YOURS
PET PEEVE: HAVING HIS EARS CLEANED
OWNERS: WENDY AND KEVIN MORROW
FAVORITE TOY: ANYTHING WITH A LOUD SQUEAK
NAUGHTIEST DEED: PULLING THE END OF THE TOILET PAPER ROLL SO PAPER GOES THROUGHOUT THE ENTIRE HOUSE
FAVORITE PASTIME: SINGIN' THE BLUES TO PIANO ACCOMPANIMENT

THORTON

OWNERS: WENDY AND KEVIN MORROW
OBSESSION: RIPPING APART PRESLEY'S TOYS AND STEALING SQUEAKERS OUT THEM
PET PEEVE: WEARING ALL THE HATS THAT WENDY MAKES
FAVORITE TOY: ANYTHING OF PRESLEY'S (RIPPED UP OF COURSE)
NAUGHTIEST DEED: GETTING PRESLEY TO SNEAK OUT OF THE GATE
FAVORITE PASTIMES: GOING FOR WALKS AND RUNNING FASTER THAN PRESLEY

ANGUS

OBSESSION: CORKS
PET PEEVES: DIVA AND JACK CAT
OWNERS: MICHAEL AND AMY SCHOLZ
NAUGHTIEST DEED: CLIMBING ONTO THE DESK AND STANDING ON THE KEYBOARD WHEN LEFT ALONE IN THE OFFICE
FAVORITE FOODS: CAT FOOD AND CARROTS
FAVORITE PASTIME: RIDING ON THE 4-WHEELER

ST. SUPÉRY ESTATE RUTHERFORD, CA | *BOXER, 6 MONTHS*

FAVORITE FOOD: FRESH PEAS
FAVORITE PASTIME: CUDDLING
OBSESSION: NOT BEING LEFT BEHIND
FAVORITE TOY: HER STUFFED LOBSTER
OWNERS: EMMA SWAIN AND WES JONES
PET PEEVE: NOT HAVING DINNER EXACTLY ON TIME
KNOWN ACCOMPLICES: BUSTER, MARTIN, MURPHY AND REDD

GG

LABRADOR, 7 | **ST. SUPÉRY ESTATE** RUTHERFORD, CA

AURI

OWNER: PETER HEITZ
FAVORITE FOOD: TREATS
FAVORITE TOY: COBRA BALL
OBSESSIONS: SHEEP AND SQUIRRELS
PET PEEVES: HATS AND GREY TOYOTA TUNDRA TRUCKS
FAVORITE PASTIME: HERDING ANYTHING THAT MOVES
KNOWN ACCOMPLICE: SLINKY MALINKY AND ECLIPSE THE BARN CATS
NAUGHTIEST DEED: STALKING AND CONSUMING AN ENTIRE ASSORTMENT OF CHEESES

SODA

OBSESSION: TALKING
OWNER: PATRICK O'DELL
PET PEEVE: THE WINE TRAIN
FAVORITE FOOD: TASTING ROOM CRACKERS
FAVORITE TOY: WHATEVER AGNES IS PLAYING WITH
FAVORITE PASTIME: CHASING AFTER RABBITS AND BIRDS
NAUGHTIEST DEED: EATING THE CARROTS IN THE GARDEN

FAVORITE FOOD: BACON
PET PEEVE: THE WINE TRAIN
OWNERS: MAX AND ZOE CATALANO
FAVORITE TOY: SOPHIE THE GIRAFFE
OBSESSION: FINDING AND BARKING AT DOGS ON THE TV
NAUGHTIEST DEED: ROLLING IN THE GARDEN AFTER A SWIM IN THE POOL
FAVORITE PASTIME: CATCHING A RIDE WITH HER SISTERS IN THEIR STROLLER

AGNES

WEST HIGHLAND TERRIERS, 5 & 11 | **TURNBULL WINE CELLARS** OAKVILLE, CA

BOO

OWNER: THE MULLINS FAMILY
FAVORITE PASTIME: SLEEPING
FAVORITE TOY: THE GIANT TENNIS BALL
OBSESSION: CHASING THE TENNIS BALL
PET PEEVE: HAVING AIR BLOWN IN HIS FACE
KNOWN ACCOMPLICE: TANK THE CHIHUAHUA
FAVORITE FOOD: ANYTHING NOT NAILED DOWN

SAM

FAVORITE FOOD: DIRT
OWNER: SALLY OTTOSON
PET PEEVE: GETTING BRUSHED
OBSESSION: TRYING TO HERD THE SHEEP
FAVORITE TOY: ANYTHING TOBY'S CHEWING ON
FAVORITE PASTIME: CHEWING ON TOBY'S EARS

TOBY

OWNER: SALLY OTTOSON
FAVORITE FOOD: PICNICS
OBSESSION: FOOD, FOOD, FOOD
FAVORITE PASTIME: BEING PICNIC SUPERVISOR
NAUGHTIEST DEED: EATING THE CAT FOOD, DAILY
PET PEEVE: SOMEBODY GUARDING THE PICNIC TABLE

BEARDED COLLIE, 8 MONTHS & BEAGLE, 10 | **PACIFIC STAR WINERY** FORT BRAGG, CA

KALI

FAVORITE FOOD: CHICKEN
OWNERS: PETER AND KATIE MONDAVI
KNOWN ACCOMPLICE: ATWOOD THE HAVANESE
PET PEEVE: ANYTHING NEW AND OUT OF THE ORDINARY
FAVORITE PASTIME: GUARDING THE FAMILY AND PROPERTY
FAVORITE TOY: CHICKEN-FLAVORED NYLABONE DURA CHEW
OBSESSION: DESTROYING "INDESTRUCTIBLE" DOG CHEW TOYS
NAUGHTIEST DEEDS: CHEWING IRRIGATION HOSING AND TEARING UP LANDSCAPING

COCO

OWNERS: BEN AND TATIANA McWILLIAMS

PET PEEVE: WORKING OVERTIME

NAUGHTIEST DEED: EATING SOMEONE'S ENTIRE LUNCH WHEN THEIR BACK WAS TURNED

FAVORITE PASTIME: RIDING IN THE BACK OF A PICK-UP TRUCK AFTER A SWIM IN THE RUSSIAN RIVER

FAVORITE FOODS: PROSCIUTTO, SALAMI AND CHORIZO

OBSESSION: PICNICKERS – CAN SPOT ONE FROM A MILE AWAY

LABRADOR, 10 | **ARISTA WINERY** *HEALDSBURG, CA*

MYRNA

PET PEEVE: GETTING HER FEET WET
FAVORITE FOOD: PRIMAL DOG FOOD
OWNERS: KIM AND CHUCK CHENAULT
FAVORITE TOY: STUFFED TOY SQUIRREL
FAVORITE PASTIME: PLAYING FETCH WITH HER TOY SQUIRREL
NAUGHTIEST DEED: DIGGING UNDER THE BACKYARD FENCE FIVE TIMES
OBSESSION: TRYING TO CATCH THE LIZARDS THAT LIVE IN THE BACKYARD

MINIATURE WIREHAIRED DACHSHUND, 4 | **ST. FRANCIS WINERY AND VINEYARDS** SANTA ROSA, CA

ABBEY

PET PEEVE: FLIES
OBSESSION: CAR RIDES
FAVORITE TOY: TENNIS BALL
OWNER: ROBERT ALDRIDGE
FAVORITE PASTIME: SLEEPING
NAUGHTIEST DEED: STEALING PIZZA OFF A KITCHEN COUNTER
FAVORITE FOOD: FROSTY PAWS FROZEN TREATS

RIGGS

OBSESSION: GOING ON WALKS
OWNER: ROBERT ALDRIDGE
NAUGHTIEST DEED: GETTING INTO THE TRASH CAN
PET PEEVE: THE VACUUM CLEANER
FAVORITE PASTIME: PLAYING CHASE
FAVORITE FOOD: CHARLEE BEAR DOG TREATS
FAVORITE TOYS: STUFFED SNAKE AND TURTLE

BELLE

PET PEEVE: TV TRAYS
FAVORITE TOY: TOY RABBIT
OWNERS: KIM AND CHUCK CHENAULT
OBSESSION: GOING FOR LONG WALKS
NAUGHTIEST DEED: CHEWING A HOLE IN THE GARAGE WALL TO GET INSIDE
FAVORITE FOOD: FROZEN TURKEY NECKS
FAVORITE PASTIME: GOING FOR LONG WALKS

 ST. FRANCIS WINERY AND VINEYARDS SANTA ROSA, CA | SWISS MOUNTAIN DOG, 8, SHIH TZU X, 8 MONTHS & KELPIE, 11

AVA

OWNER: ANDY HALEY
FAVORITE TOY: ORANGES
PET PEEVE: BEING ON A LEASH
NAUGHTIEST DEED: FOLLOWING HER NOSE
OBSESSIONS: BIRDS AND ALWAYS BEING RIGHT
FAVORITE PASTIMES: FOLLOWING HER NOSE AND POINTING
FAVORITE FOODS: YOGURT AND ANYTHING TO DO WITH PEANUT BUTTER

WIREHAIRED POINTING GRIFFON, 2 | **BOUCHAINE VINEYARDS** *NAPA, CA*

FRANKIE

FAVORITE TOY: BALL
FAVORITE FOOD: KIBBLE
NAUGHTIEST DEED: CHEWING
OBSESSION: CHASING HIS BALL
OWNERS: MARK AND TRACY DONATI
FAVORITE PASTIME: PLAYING FETCH
PET PEEVE: NOT BEING ALLOWED ON THE COUCH

VITO

FAVORITE TOY: RAWHIDE
PET PEEVE: BEING TOLD NO
OBSESSION: STEALING SHOES
FAVORITE PASTIME: NAPPING
FAVORITE FOOD: HUMAN FOOD
OWNERS: MARK AND TRACY DONATI
NAUGHTIEST DEED: JUMPING ON FURNITURE

ZINFANDEL

OBSESSIONS: BONES AND SHOES
OWNERS: MARCY AND GARY EBERLE
PET PEEVE: CATS THAT DON'T PLAY WITH HIM
FAVORITE FOODS: SHOES, TOWELS AND BONES
FAVORITE PASTIMES: CHEWING, EATING, LICKING, CHEWING, EATING, SLEEPING
NAUGHTIEST DEED: SNEAKING OUT AND FALLING INTO THE WASTEWATER POND

STANDARD POODLE, 4 MONTHS | **EBERLE WINERY** PASO ROBLES, CA

"The noblest dog of all is the hot dog:
It feeds the hand that bites it."

LAURENCE J. PETER

the GHOST WINERIES

by Jack Burton

WHEN YOU VISIT NORTHERN CALIFORNIA, keep your eyes peeled – you might find a Ghost Winery.

The term "Ghost Winery" refers to the many wineries established in the Gold Rush days before 1890, and then for reasons of vine disease or economics were left derelict.

Ghost Wineries are scattered here and there all around the wine country that lies north of the Golden Gate. Sometimes you see only the skeleton of an old estate, the falling down fruit trees and rows of ancient vines laid out like bleached bones around the footprint of an old stone structure. More often, nowadays, you might find a Ghost Winery fully restored and welcoming you to sample their delicious wines.

After the gold boom was over, and phylloxera had wasted the vines, the disaster of the Volstead Act doomed most of California's wineries in the early 1920s. A handful of vintners managed to survive Prohibition by one means or another, but the majority of family wineries simply failed.
All the effort, the vines and the grand or simple structures were simply abandoned to the bats and the barn owls.

The Spirit Dog of the Ghost Winery Commune

Uncle Buck says The Dog was "embrujado" (bewitched). Or perhaps he was a disembodied ancestor doing time back in our world. No one knew for sure, but Buck did know that the locals give him plenty of respect. Buck swears that The Dog was the same jimson weed-chewing, telepathic spirit being that had been in residence at the Ghost Winery since the early 1950s.

The Dog had come up from Texas with Ruby in an old green pickup. Ruby, The Dog and the truck had come part and parcel with the ruined old Northern California winery when Uncle Buck had purchased the place back in 1971.

Uncle Buck is a wildly bohemian fellow who had made a ton of money back in the 1960s by promoting free trade and entrepreneurship in Latin America.

When Uncle Buck signed the papers for the Ghost Winery, he also became the Jolly Benefactor to a very spirited community that was developing around Ruby and The Dog. In its hippie heyday, over 30 people were calling the Ghost Winery home.

They had all come by one connection or another to share a love of food and wine on Buck's old property. The place, the times, and the people of the commune were all ripe for new beginnings!

Ruby and The Dog provided practical and spiritual guidance as the new folks at Ghost Winery enthusiastically expanded Ruby's gardens and tended to the old vines, some of which had been planted in the days of the California Gold Rush.

Ruby was locally famous for her winemaking, and was also a Medicine Woman held in high regard by her neighbors. She had developed a unique spiritual philosophy by borrowing freely from a bewildering number of cultural sources and combining them with her own Native American traditions. She had a detailed knowledge of plant medicine, and an ability to divine a clear course of action in times of trouble or confusion.

It was also rumored that The Dog was her intermediary to the spirit realms. It was assumed The Dog had the ear of Coyote and was able to intervene at any gate or crossroad. Buck was convinced that The Dog could see over the horizon of our everyday, moment-to-moment existence. The Dog seemed always one step ahead, and Ruby consulted him regularly for all manner of advice.

One time back in the mid-1970s, on a visit to the commune at Ghost Winery, Buck found The Dog in his usual spot, sitting in the shotgun seat of Ruby's old truck. His ears were up and he looked like he was ready to travel.

Buck gave him a nice pat on the head and a good morning back scratch and asked:

"So, where do you think you're off to?"

The Dog looked him straight in the eye and crystal clear, this popped into his head: "It's time to gather the dreaming tea."... Now, that's a line to roll around in your brain-pan a few times while the breakfast is cooking! Uncle Buck was only mildly surprised when Ruby announced at the table that she and The Dog were leaving for a few weeks on the road to gather the plants and herbs essential to her craft.

Ruby, The Dog and the truck are long gone now from Ghost Winery. The winery itself has a new name and new owners who are careful to preserve the good vibes the place had acquired. People say that the Spirit Dog's presence can still be perceived in the many generations of puppies descended from his years of carrying on with the neighbor dogs.

Just last week Uncle Buck was out to picnic in the vineyards when a winery dog ambled over to the table. He gave him a nice pat on the head and a scratch behind the ears. Buck was just thinking how this dog reminded him of Ruby's old Spirit Dog when the crazy thing looked him straight in the eye and, clear as a bell, this pops into his head: "Why *that* cabernet?"

Buck was only mildly surprised when he opened his picnic wine to find the bottle was hopelessly corked.

JACK BURTON IS A WELL-TRAVELED CHEF/AUTHOR WHO LIVES AND WORKS WITH HIS PICNIC PARTNER JANETTE IN HEALDSBURG, SONOMA COUNTY, CALIFORNIA. HAVING WRITTEN A NUMBER OF AMUSING GUIDEBOOKS TO CALIFORNIA WINE COUNTRY, JACK IS ALSO AN ACCOMPLISHED SILVERSMITH — WWW.LAZYSUMMERTRADERS.COM
THIS STORY HAS BEEN REPRINTED FROM *WINE DOGS USA*, PUBLISHED 2006.

MAC

FAVORITE FOOD: SALMON
OWNERS: PRISCILLA AND ROGER HIGGINS
OBSESSIONS: TENNIS BALLS AND TENNIS BALLS
FAVORITE PASTIMES: TEACHING HIS OWNERS NEW GAMES
KNOWN ACCOMPLICES: CHLOE AND CLEO, HIS CALICO CATS
PET PEEVE: CLEO, THE CAT, CHASING AND CATCHING HIS TAIL
NAUGHTIEST DEED: HERDING THE UPS TRUCK AND BITING ITS TIRES

BORDER COLLIE, 10 | **CIMARONE WINES** *LOS OLIVOS, CA*

LULU KATE

OWNER: JESSICA LUBERS
FAVORITE TOY: TOY DUCK
OBSESSION: PLAYING FETCH
NAUGHTIEST DEED: DIGGING IN THE YARD
KNOWN ACCOMPLICE: HER BEST FRIEND PONCHO
FAVORITE PASTIME: RUNNING THROUGH THE VINEYARDS

FRENCHIE III

FAVORITE TOY: HIS MASERATI
OWNER: JEAN-CHARLES BOISSET
FAVORITE PASTIME: CHASING AFTER SEXY LADY DOGS IN FRENCHIE WINERY
FAVORITE FOOD: FOIE GRAS, OF COURSE
PET PEEVE: DOGS WITH NO PASSION FOR WINE
KNOWN ACCOMPLICES: CITEAUX AND FRENCHIE II

RUBY RED BEAR

OBSESSION: BALLS
FAVORITE FOOD: DOG BONES
OWNERS: JIM AND NANCY BUNDSCHU
PET PEEVE: NOT GETTING ENOUGH ATTENTION
NAUGHTIEST DEED: DROPPING SLOPPY WET BALLS IN YOUR LAP
FAVORITE PASTIMES: TAKING HIKES WITH JIM AND CHASING BALLS

BACCHUS B.

OWNER: KATIE BUNDSCHU
OBSESSION: DIGGING FOR GOPHERS
KNOWN ACCOMPLICE: RUBY RED BEAR
FAVORITE FOOD: ANYTHING BUT DOG FOOD
PET PEEVE: NOT GETTING ENOUGH PLAYTIME
FAVORITE PASTIME: BARKING AT THE DONKEYS
NAUGHTIEST DEED: DRAGGING KATIE INTO THE POND

ABBIE

OWNERS: JOHN AND TORI WILLIAMS

KNOWN ACCOMPLICES: ELLIE THE CAT, SKITTLES THE BIRD AND BUSTER WHO SENDS A VALENTINE EACH YEAR

NAUGHTIEST DEED: COOLING OFF IN THE WINERY POND THEN SHAKING OFF ON THE WINERY DECK IN FRONT OF GUESTS

PET PEEVE: PEOPLE WHO DON'T FINISH THEIR TASTING WINE

OBSESSIONS: CHASING THE CAT AND GUARDING THE CHICKENS AT HOME

FAVORITE TOY: ANY FRUIT FROM THE ORCHARD THAT CAN DOUBLE AS A BALL

WIREHAIRED POINTING GRIFFON, 5 | **FROG'S LEAP** RUTHERFORD, CA

LADY

PET PEEVE: TURKEYS
FAVORITE TOY: STICKS
FAVORITE FOOD: ROAST CHICKEN
NAUGHTIEST DEED: TAKING A LEG OF LAMB OFF THE COUNTER AND EATING IT
OWNERS: LYNN SAKASEGAWA AND PAUL STOKES
FAVORITE PASTIMES: PLAYING WITH STICKS AND GOING ON WALKS

KAYA

OBSESSION: PEOPLE
OWNER: ANDREA DE PALO
PET PEEVE: BEING DRESSED UP
NAUGHTIEST DEED: BEGGING FOR FOOD WHEN GUESTS ARE ON THE PATIO
FAVORITE TOY: STICK FROM AN OLD VINE
FAVORITE PASTIMES: LAYING IN THE GARDEN OR FROLICKING IN THE VINEYARDS
KNOWN ACCOMPLICE: UNCLE CJ IN THE TASTING ROOM

RUBY

OWNER: TOY CANTO
NAUGHTIEST DEED: EATING A FROG
OBSESSION: NIGHT-TIME GLOWBALL
FAVORITE TOY: SQUISHY WORLD BALL
FAVORITE FOODS: DUCK BREAST AND PASTA
PET PEEVE: BEING LEFT HOME TO GUARD THE CAT
FAVORITE PASTIME: TAGGING ALONG FOR A RIDE WITH HER HORSE BUDDIES SHINER AND JOE BLACK

KAYA

FAVORITE FOOD: SALMON SKIN
OWNERS: LUCAS AND NICOLE POPE
FAVORITE TOY: WINE BARREL BUNGS
OBSESSIONS: DEER AND SQUIRRELS
PET PEEVE: BEING LEFT AT HOME ON A WORK DAY
FAVORITE PASTIMES: PLAYING FETCH AND SWIMMING
NAUGHTIEST DEED: ROLLING IN HOMEMADE FISH EMULSION

PHOEBE

FAVORITE FOOD: SALAD
OWNERS: MITCH AND LESLIE WYSS
FAVORITE TOY: THE FUNKY MONKEY
NAUGHTIEST DEED: COUNTER SURFING
OBSESSION: CHASING INVISIBLE THINGS
PET PEEVE: CATS MOVING THROUGH HER TURF
FAVORITE PASTIMES: ROARING AROUND AND SHOWING OFF

SLATE

NAUGHTIEST DEED: SOCK THIEVERY
OWNERS: DARREN AND DESIREE RAMOS
FAVORITE PASTIME: COUNTER SURFING
OBSESSIONS: CHASING DEER AND HUNTING GOPHERS
FAVORITE TOY: ANY TOY THAT RESULTS IN TUG-OF-WAR
PET PEEVES: TEENAGERS WITH HOODIES AND SKATEBOARDS

HALTER RANCH VINEYARD PASO ROBLES, CA | AUSTRALIAN SHEPHERD, 2

ROCKY

OBSESSION: FOOD
FAVORITE TOY: A DE-STUFFED FOX
OWNERS: CRAIG AND KATHRYN HALL
NAUGHTIEST DEED: FORGETTING HE IS INSIDE
PET PEEVE: WAITING TILL COCO FINISHES HER MEAL
FAVORITE PASTIME: CHASING AFTER COCO WHEN SHE CHASES BALLS

COCO

OBSESSION: TENNIS BALLS
OWNERS: CRAIG AND KATHRYN HALL
FAVORITE FOOD: ANYTHING HANDFED
PET PEEVE: INTRUDERS IN THE HOUSE
FAVORITE PASTIME: CHASING AFTER BALLS
NAUGHTIEST DEED: BARKING AT 4AM AT COYOTES

ROMEO

OWNERS: MATTHEW AND CHRISTINA BEVERLY
PET PEEVES: FOOTBALL AND BEING SNUGGLED TOO LONG
FAVORITE FOODS: BACON AND ANYTHING FOUND ON THE GROUND
OBSESSION: HAVING TO FOLLOW CHRISTINA EVERYWHERE INSIDE THE HOUSE
NAUGHTIEST DEED: PEEING ON A CHIHUAHUA WHILE MARKING HIS TERRITORY
FAVORITE PASTIME: RUNNING ALONGSIDE WHILE MATT LONGBOARDS AROUND TOWN
KNOWN ACCOMPLICES: THE LITTLE LEBOWSKI (HIS CAT) AND LUNA (HIS GOLDENDOODLE LADY FRIEND)

HONEY

OWNER: ANGELA DOUGLASS
FAVORITE FOOD: TASTING ROOM CRACKERS
PET PEEVE: DELIVERY MEN WITHOUT DOG BISCUITS
OBSESSIONS: FULL MOONS AND HOT AIR BALLOONS
FAVORITE TOY: ANYTHING STUFFED THAT HAS A TAIL
NAUGHTIEST DEED: CHASING DOWN DELIVERY TRUCKS
FAVORITE PASTIME: LEADING VINEYARD TOURS WITH GEORGE HENDRY

CHIWEENIE, 2 | **HENDRY RANCH WINERY** NAPA, CA

SAMPSON

FAVORITE FOOD: CHEESE
FAVORITE PASTIME: DIGGING
FAVORITE TOY: TENNIS BALLS
OWNERS: PAUL AND MEGHAN HAWLEY
NAUGHTIEST DEED: DIGGING UP THE LAWN
PET PEEVE: LOSING HIS BALL UNDER THE COUCH
OBSESSION: DIGGING FOR GOPHERS IN THE VINEYARD
KNOWN ACCOMPLICE: AMOS FROM SANGLIER CELLARS

RANGER

OWNER: KATHY METTLER
PET PEEVE: GETTING LICKED ON THE NOSE BY THE CAT, ALBI
FAVORITE PASTIME: GREETING CUSTOMERS AT THE WINERY
FAVORITE FOOD: BBQ SAUSAGE
OBSESSION: KYLE, WHO TAKES HIM TO WORK IN THE VINEYARDS
NAUGHTIEST DEED: CLEARING AN APPETIZER PLATTER BEING USED FOR A PHOTO SHOOT

LITTLE LILY

FAVORITE TOY: SOCCER BALL
OBSESSION: HERDING CARS
OWNERS: SUSAN AND DAVE GARRETSON
FAVORITE FOODS: CHEESE AND DRY SALAMI
FAVORITE PASTIME: FOLLOWING BUDDY AROUND
PET PEEVE: NOT BEING ALLOWED IN THE TASTING ROOM
NAUGHTIEST DEED: RUNNING UNDER CARS AND SCARING THE DRIVERS

BUDDY LOVE

FAVORITE FOOD: PIZZA
FAVORITE TOYS: STICKS AND FIREWOOD
OWNERS: SUSAN AND DAVE GARRETSON
FAVORITE PASTIME: CARRYING STICKS, LOGS AND ROCKS
OBSESSIONS: HUNTING BIRDS, CHASING CARS AND CARRYING THINGS IN HIS MOUTH
NAUGHTIEST DEED: STEALING THE FIREWOOD AND CARRYING IT AROUND THE PROPERTY

BOSCO

OBSESSION: COUNTER SURFING
PET PEEVE: THE VET TAKING HIS TEMPERATURE
FAVORITE PASTIMES: HIKING AND PLAYING BALL
FAVORITE FOODS: LAMB AND JUNIPER BERRIES
OWNERS: KATHRYN CINQUE AND STEPHEN ROSENTHAL
NAUGHTIEST DEED: CHEWING UP THE BACK OF TWO CARS

LILY

OWNER: ALEC HODGDON
OBSESSION: RETRIEVING
FAVORITE TOY: TENNIS BALL
PET PEEVE: GOING OUT IN THE RAIN
FAVORITE FOODS: HOT DOGS AND LIVER TREATS
NAUGHTIEST DEED: USING A LIGHT BULB AS A CHEW TOY

HALLIE

OWNER: JOHN CONOVER
NAUGHTIEST DEED: THIEVERY
FAVORITE FOOD: BEEF STICKS OUT OF THE BIN AT FIDEAUX IN ST. HELENA
OBSESSION: BEGGING AND, WHEN THAT FAILS, STEALING FOOD FROM THE UNSUSPECTING
PET PEEVE: WHEN A PERSON SITS ON HER SECTION OF THE COUCH
FAVORITE PASTIME: RIDING IN THE FRONT SEAT OF THE PICK-UP TRUCK

MOLLY

FAVORITE TOY: TUG-OF-WAR ROPE
PET PEEVE: DRY FOXTAILS (PLANTS)
OWNERS: MARLA AND DALE BLEECHER
FAVORITE FOODS: DOG BISCUITS AND LEFTOVER BONES
OBSESSION: BARKING AT IMAGINED AND REAL OUTSIDE NOISES
NAUGHTIEST DEED: 'DRYING OFF' FROM A BATH IN A FRESH COW PIE
FAVORITE PASTIME: SLEEPING ON THE CONCRETE FLOOR IN THE MIDDLE OF THE WINERY

DAGGER TOOTH

OBSESSION: MOLLY
FAVORITE FOOD: CHEESE
PET PEEVES: HOT OR RAINY WEATHER
OWNERS: MARLA AND DALE BLEECHER
FAVORITE PASTIME: FETCHING TENNIS BALLS
FAVORITE TOY: TENNIS BALLS OF ALL SHAPES AND SIZES
NAUGHTIEST DEED: CONTINUALLY TAKING HIS MOTHER BACCI'S BED

BACCI

OBSESSION: TENNIS BALLS
NAUGHTIEST DEED: PICKING A FIGHT WITH A MUCH LARGER NEIGHBOR'S DOG
OWNERS: MARLA AND DALE BLEECHER
PET PEEVES: RAIN, SURPRISES AND STAIRS
FAVORITE PASTIME: FETCHING TENNIS BALLS
FAVORITE TOY: TENNIS BALLS OF ALL SHAPES AND SIZES

BLU

OBSESSIONS: WALKS AND FOOD
PET PEEVE: HAVING HIS FEET TOUCHED
FAVORITE TOYS: HOOT OWL AND HIS BED
OWNERS: MICHELE AND JOHN ANTHONY TRUCHARD
FAVORITE FOOD: ANYTHING THAT STARTS WITH "F" (AS IN "FOOD")
NAUGHTIEST DEED: CHEWING THROUGH MICHELE'S LEATHER SANDALS
FAVORITE PASTIME: EATING SNACKS THAT FALL FROM THE BREAKFAST TABLE

LUE

OBSESSION: LICKING
NAUGHTIEST DEED: SMASHING A CASE OF ROSÉ THEN LICKING IT ALL UP
OWNERS: AMANDA AND DAMIAN GRINDLEY
PET PEEVE: FLYING BACK AND FORTH TO AUSTRALIA
FAVORITE PASTIME: SWIMMING IN PEOPLE'S POOLS
FAVORITE FOODS: PIES, PASTIES AND SAUSAGE ROLLS

ROY

FAVORITE TOY: SQUEAKY SQUIRREL
OWNERS: AMANDA AND DAMIAN GRINDLEY
FAVORITE PASTIME: CHEWING ON LUE'S TAIL
PET PEEVE: NOT BEING ALLOWED TO SIT RIGHT ON TOP OF YOU
NAUGHTIEST DEED: CHEWING ON THE NEW SOFA, BED AND TABLE

CANON

OBSESSION: SQUIRRELS
FAVORITE FOOD: BIRDSEED
PET PEEVE: CHATTERING SQUIRRELS
OWNERS: JENNIFER AND MICHAEL KEENAN
FAVORITE TOY: STUFFING FROM A SQUIRREL TOY
FAVORITE PASTIMES: RUNNING AND SQUIRREL CHASING
NAUGHTIEST DEED: CLIMBING TREES (AFTER SQUIRRELS)

BANDIT

OBSESSION: FOOD
FAVORITE TOY: SNACKS
KNOWN ACCOMPLICE: CANON
OWNERS: JENNIFER AND MICHAEL KEENAN
NAUGHTIEST DEED: BEING A GARBAGE HOUND
FAVORITE PASTIMES: SLEEPING AND SNIFFING ABOUT

SCRAPPY

OWNER: LAURA MARCH
FAVORITE TOY: ANYTHING STUFFED
OBSESSION: CHEESE AND CRACKERS
FAVORITE PASTIMES: LOUNGING AROUND ALL DAY AND CHASING FOXES AT NIGHT
FAVORITE FOODS: CHEESE AND CRACKERS
PET PEEVE: NOT BEING ABLE TO CATCH A FOX
NAUGHTIEST DEED: EATING CAT FOOD (DAILY)

MIRA

FAVORITE TOY: GIANT ORANGE BALL
FAVORITE FOOD: VANILLA ICE-CREAM
OWNERS: MATT AND SHARI GARDNER
FAVORITE PASTIME: PLAYING IN THE WATER
OBSESSIONS: BUBBLES AND LIGHT REFLECTIONS
NAUGHTIEST DEED: PLAYING ON THE WINERY ROOF
KNOWN ACCOMPLICES: SCRAPPY AND NUTTER BUTTER THE KITTEN

KEENAN WINERY ST. HELENA, CA | BORDER COLLIE X, 3

MILO

NAUGHTIEST DEED: EATING GRAPES DURING THE HARVEST
OBSESSION: GETTING ALL THE ATTENTION
FAVORITE TOY: SQUEAKY STUFFED EGGPLANT
FAVORITE PASTIME: PLAYING BALL
PET PEEVE: THE LAWNMOWER
FAVORITE FOOD: TOMATOES
OWNER: SARAH McCREA

COCKER SPANIEL, 12 | **STONY HILL VINEYARD** ST. HELENA, CA

"Great men have great dogs."

OTTO VON BISMARCK

LUCE

FAVORITE FOOD: CHICKEN
FAVORITE TOY: A PLUSH MOLE
PET PEEVES: DARKNESS AND RAIN
FAVORITE PASTIME: PLAYING WITH MALBEC
OWNERS: ROBERT AND MARGRIT MONDAVI
KNOWN ACCOMPLICES: ROBERT AND MARGRIT
NAUGHTIEST DEED: DIGGING INTO SHEETS AND PILLOWS

ROBERT MONDAVI

FAVORITE TOY: LUCE
FAVORITE FOOD: PASTA
PET PEEVE: BEING LATE
FAVORITE PASTIMES: A NICE MEAL WITH FRIENDS, GOOD WINE AND GOOD FOOD
NAUGHTIEST DEED: FLIRTING WITH PRETTY WOMEN
KNOWN ACCOMPLICES: MARGRIT, VINTNERS AND ARTISTS

COCO

PET PEEVE: BATHTIME
OWNERS: DAN AND ALLI KOSTA
NAUGHTIEST DEED: PASSING GAS
FAVORITE PASTIME: LICKING PEOPLE
FAVORITE FOOD: CHICKEN EGGS FROM THE COOP
FAVORITE TOYS: MAZIE, MAGGIE AND SEAN
OBSESSIONS: CHASING DEER AND SLEEPING
KNOWN ACCOMPLICES: SWITCH AND BUDDY

JADE

FAVORITE FOOD: PORK
FAVORITE TOY: TENNIS BALLS
FAVORITE PASTIME: PLAYING FETCH
PET PEEVE: NOT BEING PLAYED WITH
OWNERS: MICHAEL AND SARAH BROWNE
NAUGHTIEST DEED: PEEING ON THE GRASS
OBSESSIONS: HER FAMILY AND CHEWING ON THINGS

LOLLY

PET PEEVE: THE WORD "NO"
FAVORITE FOOD: CHICKEN
OWNER: MARCIA KUNDE MICKELSON
OBSESSION: TRYING TO HERD PEOPLE, ESPECIALLY IF THEY ARE WEARING BOOTS
FAVORITE TOY: BIG BROWN FURRY MONKEY
NAUGHTIEST DEED: PULLING OUT GERANIUMS
FAVORITE PASTIME: LOUNGING UNDER MARCIA'S DESK

JACKIE

OWNER: JIM MICKELSON
PET PEEVE: BEING LEFT AT HOME
FAVORITE TOYS: BLUE RUBBER PUPPY AND THE OCCASIONAL TURKEY
FAVORITE FOODS: BACON AND CHICKEN
FAVORITE PASTIME: HERDING COWS WITH JIM
OBSESSION: SHAKING THE TAR OUT OF HER TOYS

REMI

FAVORITE TOY: DONUT
OWNER: JENNA KUNDE
OBSESSION: JEFF KUNDE
FAVORITE PASTIMES: LOUNGING ON THE PORCH AND SWIMMING IN THE LAKE
PET PEEVE: HAVING HER PAWS TOUCHED
NAUGHTIEST DEED: GETTING INTO THE TRASH

PET PEEVE: PUPPIES
OWNERS: RYAN AND JESSICA CARR
OBSESSION: PLAYING AT THE BEACH
FAVORITE FOODS: BURRITOS AND PIZZA
FAVORITE PASTIME: GREETING CUSTOMERS AT THE WINERY
KNOWN ACCOMPLICE: THE COYOTE THAT LIVES AT PAREDON VINEYARD
NAUGHTIEST DEED: STEALING A WHOLE CHICKEN OFF SOMEONE'S PLATE AT THE PARK

ROXY

ELLIE

OBSESSION: BELLY RUBS
FAVORITE FOOD: OLIVES FALLEN FROM THE TREES AT BLACKBIRD VINEYARDS
FAVORITE TOY: MICHAEL AND KIMBERLY'S SOCKS
OWNERS: MICHAEL POLENSKE AND KIMBERLY MILLER

WILEY

OBSESSION: FOOD OF ANY KIND
PET PEEVE: STRANGERS AT THE DOOR
FAVORITE PASTIME: SNUGGLING WITH MICHAEL AND KIMBERLY IN BED IN THE MORNING
OWNERS: MICHAEL POLENSKE AND KIMBERLY MILLER
NAUGHTIEST DEED: TEARING APART HIS 'PIDDLE PADS' WHEN LEFT ALONE

PETE

PET PEEVE: BATH TIME
FAVORITE TOY: HUMANS
KNOWN ACCOMPLICE: SUNNY
OWNERS: TOM AND BECKY LARSON
FAVORITE FOOD: WHATEVER YOU'RE HAVING
FAVORITE PASTIME: SWIMMING IN SONOMA CREEK

BUSTER

FAVORITE FOOD: TREATS
PET PEEVE: LOUD TRUCKS
FAVORITE TOY: SQUEAKY TOYS
OWNERS: TOM AND BECKY LARSON
NAUGHTIEST DEED: BEING AN ESCAPE ARTIST
FAVORITE PASTIME: NAPPING IN THE TASTING ROOM

BUBBA

OBSESSION: BALLS
FAVORITE TOY: BALLS
FAVORITE FOOD: PEANUT BUTTER
OWNERS: TOM AND BECKY LARSON
PET PEEVE: BEING WITHOUT HIS BALL
FAVORITE PASTIME: BEING IN THE VINEYARD WITH ISIDRO, THE VINEYARD MANAGER

SCARLET

OWNER: CAT KAISER
PET PEEVE: CAR WASHES
OBSESSION: LOOKING STRAIGHT INTO YOUR EYES
FAVORITE TOY: SCOOTER, HER FOUR-FOOT SOCK MONKEY
FAVORITE PASTIME: BEING AS CLOSE AS POSSIBLE TO CAT
FAVORITE FOODS: WINERY BREADSTICKS AND BABY CARROTS
NAUGHTIEST DEED: POOPING IN THE CAR WHILE GOING THROUGH A CAR WASH

LEDSON WINERY AND VINEYARDS *KENWOOD, CA* | *GOLDENDOODLE, 5*

PISTOL

OWNER: STEVE LEDSON
FAVORITE TOY: NOISY FIRE TRUCK
OBSESSIONS: FRISBEES AND HUNTING
NAUGHTIEST DEED: DISAPPEARING FOR HOURS CHASING RABBITS IN THE VINEYARD
FAVORITE FOODS: FILET MIGNON AND PROTEIN BARS
PET PEEVE: PEOPLE RIDING IN THE FRONT SEAT OF HER TRUCK

From left:

MISS ELLIE: FAVORITE FOOD: ANYTHING EXCEPT CHIPS
PET PEEVE: CHUY (WHEN HE IS BEING NEEDY)
OWNER: RON NICHOLSEN

CHUY: NAUGHTIEST DEED: CHEWING LAUREN'S SHOES
PET PEEVE: RON'S RINGTONE
('PRINCE OF DARKNESS' BY OZZY OSBOURNE)
OWNERS: RON AND LAUREN NICHOLSEN

GABBY: PET PEEVE: HAM'S WIFE, DIONE
OBSESSION: MAKING OUT WITH HAM
OWNER: HAMILTON NICHOLSEN

AL PASTOR: OBSESSION: HORSE POO
FAVORITE PASTIME: SHREDDING
ANY CASH FOUND IN THE CAR
OWNER: DIONE CARSTON

RED BONE COONHOUND, 5, CHIHUAHUA X, 5, LABRADOR, 7 & CHIHUAHUA X, 1 | **KELHAM VINEYARDS** ST. HELENA, CA

REMINGTON

FAVORITE TOY: BALLS
OWNER: JANET TREFETHEN
OBSESSION: MAKING SURE EVERYONE IN THE TASTING ROOM GIVES HER ATTENTION
FAVORITE FOOD: AUSTRALIAN LIVER TREATS
PET PEEVE: PEOPLE WHO LOOK AT THE BALL BUT DON'T THROW IT
NAUGHTIEST DEED: DISAPPEARING INTO THE HILLS WHEN SHE WAS A PUPPY

FAVORITE FOOD: LEAVES
OWNER: ASHLEY BRANDNER
FAVORITE TOY: HIS ELK ANTLER
FAVORITE PASTIME: PESTERING GRIFFIN
OBSESSIONS: BIRDS AND ANYTHING ON THE MOVE
PET PEEVE: NOT BEING THE CENTER OF ATTENTION
NAUGHTIEST DEED: EATING FURNITURE AND LADIES' UNDERGARMENTS

PEPÉ

SHEPADOODLE, 11 MONTHS | **JESSUP CELLARS** YOUNTVILLE, CA

KLINKER

FAVORITE FOOD: BACON
FAVORITE PASTIME: PLAYING WITH HIS BLUE RACQUETBALL
OWNER: FARRAH FELTEN JOLLEY
NAUGHTIEST DEED: LICKING LIPS
PET PEEVE: EMPTY WINE GLASSES
FAVORITE TOY: STUFFED BUNNY RABBIT
KNOWN ACCOMPLICE: VINNIE THE CHIWEENIE
OBSESSION: BEING THE CENTER OF ATTENTION

HARRY the SOMMELIER DOG

by Jennifer Rosen

AS A TEENAGER, I lived for a few years on a large farm owned by my Great Aunt Laura. She was what was once known as a spinster and an heiress, but people caught up in her whirlwind just called her unique.

In place of family, she had a stable full of horses, and a large pack of dogs. Breeds went in and out, but the leashes, chains and collars that were an integral part of her fashion statement stayed the same.

A short, stylish woman, Aunt Laura stood ramrod straight and walked very fast with an odd toe-to-heel placement that was considered healthful at the time. Late afternoons would find her striding for miles across her land, clinking with chains, whips and leashes and surrounded by a pack of what looked like a dozen wolves. Woe to the trespasser who got within range. "Who are you?" my aunt would demand as the hapless fellow cowered up a tree, "And what do you think you're doing here?" After she was quite certain the guy had wet his pants she'd begin talking to him about shark fossils in the stream, or wild mushrooms in the woods and pretty soon he'd have an open invitation to visit.

By the time I arrived the pack was mostly German Weimaraners, the long-haired kind. If you've never seen these, imagine a large Golden Retriever with a muddy-grey coat and yellow-green eyes. Aunt Laura was wild about both these colors, as one look at her car, house and clothes would tell you. Unfortunately for my opportunity to own exquisite designer hand-me-downs, I happen to look deathly in those colors. But that's another story.

Now, due to some accident of breeding, in the midst of all this fur was one short-hair named Harry. Harry was the most elegant dog I've ever seen. He moved with a suspended, gravity-defying trot, and stood with what Irish horse-traders call "a leg at each corner." His soulful, wide-set eyes and high head carriage struck a note between noble and haughty.

Harry had a special set of rain gear, made to measure for him in Scotland; a beautiful trench coat with epaulettes and tartan lining plus a matching hat and boots, although these never stayed on long because for some reason, Harry couldn't stand to have his paws touched. You could run your finger over the top of his foot and he'd snatch it right up. We never knew why, but it only added to his fastidious air.

All in all, he reminded me of the head-butler in a grand English country house, or the kind of sommelier who wears a silver tastevin on a chain and makes you quake when it's your turn to taste and pronounce judgment on that first pour.

There was one chink in Harry's armor. He had fixed his amorous attentions upon a psychedelic purple paisley Superball, about the size of your fist. He kept it in his mouth all day, sometimes chewing, sometimes just holding it in his jaw and mouthing it lovingly. He would only drop it when it was time to eat. But of course when you drop a Superball it rebounds all over the place, like into all the other dogs busy wolfing down their dinner. Harry would go through this agonizing choice of whether to rescue his beloved or defend his kibble.

This would have been more of a wine story except that Aunt Laura didn't really drink. Unless you want to count those few special occasions when she'd "take" a tiny glass of Lillet. But admirers and former trespassers who didn't know this would often show up bearing a bottle, which would be promptly locked in the liquor closet, a small cubby under the stairs.

As I got older and began learning about wine, it began to irk me that not only were the bottles kept in a space that could go over 90 degrees on a summer night, but, worse, they were all kept standing up. In those pre-screwcap days, that meant a lot of dried-up corks and spoiled wine. So one day I sat down in front of the closet and carefully lay all the bottles down on their sides. A few days later, Aunt Laura went noodling through the house and stood them all back up.

I explained all about corks and seals, but she thought the bottles looked messy on the floor. Over and over I'd sneak in and set them down, and she'd find out and stand them all up again.

Then one day – I wasn't there, and my aunt told me about this later – she came upon Harry standing at the door to the liquor closet, scratching the floor, sniffing the door and whining. Figuring he must smell a mouse or a rat, she unlocked the closet and as she did, Harry plunged his head in and KO'd a number of bottles before my aunt could grab his collar and haul him back.

Harry continued to paw and whine, straining against his collar. Then, he reached out one paw and with a kind of fastidious punch, he flattened a bottle of Châteauneuf-du-Pape. Curious, my aunt gave him a little more leeway with which he proceeded to knock down bottles like they were bowling pins. Finally, with a great lunge, he broke free of my aunt's grasp, thrust his head all the way into the closet, and felled the bottles left standing. Then he backed up, turned around, walked away, and sat down like nothing had happened, quietly chewing in his usual noble way.

"I had no idea what it all meant" my aunt told me later, "but he seemed so satisfied. And I couldn't help wondering if maybe he agreed with you about storing wine bottles on their sides." And from then on, not only did she leave the bottles lying, but eventually let me move them down to the cellar, where the cool temperatures were far more suitable to an aging bottle.

When she died, decades later, she left a large cellar of these gift bottles, along with a secret stash of pre-prohibition wine, all in good shape, all on its side.

At the time, though, I was just grateful to sommelier-dog Harry. So much so, in fact, that I vowed never to hide his Superball in the closet again.

THE LATE **JENNIFER ROSEN** IS THE AUTHOR OF *WAITER, THERE'S A HORSE IN MY WINE*, *THE CORK JESTER'S GUIDE TO WINE* AND A NEW GAME, *CORK JESTER'S WINE TEASERS*. SHE WROTE A WEEKLY WINE COLUMN FOR THE *ROCKY MOUNTAIN NEWS* AND ARTICLES FOR MAGAZINES AND PAPERS AROUND THE WORLD. JENNIFER SPOKE FRENCH AND ITALIAN, MANGLED GERMAN, SPANISH AND ARABIC, AND WORKED OFF THE JOB PERKS WITH BELLY DANCE, TIGHTROPE AND TRAPEZE. THIS STORY HAS BEEN REPRINTED FROM *WINE DOGS USA 2*, PUBLISHED 2008.

SPENCER

OBSESSION: BALLS
PET PEEVE: BOREDOM
FAVORITE FOOD: SLOW-BAKED YAMS
FAVORITE TOY: SQUEAKY WEASEL TOY
NAUGHTIEST DEED: SNEAKILY POOPING UNDER KEVIN'S DESK DURING A MEETING
OWNERS: TAMARA SALKA AND KEVIN KINSELLA
KNOWN ACCOMPLICE: COOPER OF SHIBUMI KNOLL
FAVORITE PASTIME: SWIMMING IN SPENCER LAKE

BISMARCK

OWNER: JOHN JORDAN
OBSESSION: PATROLLING THE WINERY LIKE A LITTLE DICTATOR
PET PEEVE: PEOPLE DEFYING HIS WISHES
FAVORITE PASTIME: WAITING AT THE WINERY KITCHEN'S BACKDOOR FOR TREATS
NAUGHTIEST DEED: BARKING UNTIL JOHN BREAKS DOWN AND GIVES HIM A TREAT

NIMITZ

OWNER: JOHN JORDAN
FAVORITE TOY: A TENNIS BALL FLOATING ON JORDAN LAKE
OBSESSION: SLEEPING BY JOHN'S FEET
PET PEEVE: HAVING HIS EARS PLAYED WITH
NAUGHTIEST DEED: PUSHING JOHN OFF THE BED
FAVORITE PASTIME: SWIMMING IN JORDAN LAKE

ROSIE

OWNER: JOHN JORDAN
OBSESSION: CHASING THE COWS AROUND THE PASTURE
FAVORITE FOOD: DANTE'S TREATS
FAVORITE PASTIMES: PATROLLING HER HOUSE AND BARKING
NAUGHTIEST DEED: BARKING AT 3AM
PET PEEVE: BEING MOVED WHEN SHE IS ASLEEP

DANTE

OWNER: LISA MATTSON
PET PEEVE: NOT GETTING TO VISIT RUBY IN ACCOUNTING AFTER HIS MORNING WALK
FAVORITE PASTIME: CHASING WILD TURKEYS
FAVORITE FOOD: REDWOOD HILL FARM YOGURT
OBSESSIONS: LISA'S RUNNING SHOES AND RUBY
FAVORITE TOYS: HIS STUFFED HEDGEHOG AND CARDBOARD TUBES
NAUGHTIEST DEED: RIPPING A CALVIN KLEIN DUVET COVER TO SHREDS

RUBY

OWNER: JULIE PARRISH
PET PEEVE: BEING LEFT AT HOME
FAVORITE FOOD: PEANUT BUTTER
FAVORITE TOY: PEANUT BUTTER-FILLED KONG
FAVORITE PASTIME: VISITING HER HUMAN FRIENDS
OBSESSION: THE END-OF-WORKDAY PEANUT BUTTER RUN TO THE OFFICE AROUND THE CORNER
NAUGHTIEST DEED: UNMAKING JULIE'S BED ON A REGULAR BASIS

MR. MATTHEWS

FAVORITE TOY: HIS HEDGEHOG
PET PEEVE: NOT BEING INVITED TO A PARTY
NAUGHTIEST DEED: BEING AN ESCAPE ARTIST
OWNERS: JODY COOKE AND DAVE CASTANEDA
KNOWN ACCOMPLICE: HIS GIRLFRIEND, PARIS
FAVORITE FOODS: BACON AND RAWHIDE BONES
FAVORITE PASTIME: LISTENING TO DAVE MATTHEWS WITH DAVE

KODA

OWNER: ANDREW PIMENTEL
FAVORITE FOOD: DUCK JERKY
PET PEEVE: SWIMMING OR BATHS
FAVORITE PASTIMES: WRESTLING AND RUNNING
NAUGHTIEST DEED: DIGGING FOR COOL DIRT OR GOPHERS
KNOWN ACCOMPLICE: GABE THE NEIGHBORING LABRADOR
OBSESSIONS: ALL OTHER DOGS AND GOING FOR CAR RIDES

BRUNO

OWNERS: TOM LEONARDINI AND FAMILY
FAVORITE FOOD: FETTUCCINE WITH PESTO
FAVORITE TOYS: DEER ANTLER AND BASEBALLS
FAVORITE PASTIMES: SLEEPING AND CHASING RABBITS
OBSESSION: STEALING STUFFED ANIMALS AND CLOTHES AND STACKING THEM UP
NAUGHTIEST DEEDS: ATTACKING GARBAGE AND STEALING FOOD OUT OF KIDS' HANDS

LUCY

OWNER: KATIE LEONARDINI
OBSESSION: COUGAR THE CAT
FAVORITE FOODS: CHEESE AND WILD DEER STICKS
NAUGHTIEST DEED: LAUNDRY BASKET DIVING FOR DIRTY SOCKS
PET PEEVES: TAKING BATHS AND GOING IN THE SWIMMING POOL
FAVORITE PASTIME: MONITORING AND CHASING THE NEIGHBORHOOD BLUE JAYS

NEWTON

OWNER: SYDNEY WILSON
OBSESSION: PEOPLE ON BIKES
FAVORITE FOOD: STRAWBERRIES
FAVORITE TOY: ANYTHING THAT SQUEAKS
NAUGHTIEST DEED: POOPING IN THE CLOSET
PET PEEVE: PEOPLE RINGING THE DOORBELL
FAVORITE PASTIMES: CHEWING SHOES AND SNUGGLING

OWNER: DIANE WILSON
PET PEEVE: BEING BRUSHED
NAUGHTIEST DEED: CHEWING
FAVORITE FOOD: WILSON WINERY TRI-TIP
FAVORITE TOYS: TUGGY TOY AND STUFFED FLAMINGO
FAVORITE PASTIMES: RUNNING AND PLAYING TUG-OF-WAR

MOLLY

ROBBIE

PET PEEVE: DOGS
FAVORITE TOYS: CUSTOMERS
OBSESSION: HOSTING GUESTS
FAVORITE FOOD: WILD SALMON
FAVORITE PASTIME: GETTING TUMMY RUBS
KNOWN ACCOMPLICES: THE KENDALL-JACKSON STAFF
OWNERS: JESS JACKSON AND BARBARA BANKE

NOELLE

FAVORITE FOOD: CAT FOOD
FAVORITE TOY: SQUEAKY TOYS
FAVORITE PASTIME: TAKING MUD BATHS
OWNERS: JESS JACKSON AND BARBARA BANKE
KNOWN ACCOMPLICES: SIENA, GORDIE AND BUDDY
OBSESSION: ROLLING IN VARIOUS UNSAVORY SUBSTANCES
NAUGHTIEST DEED: SHREDDING HOMEWORK AND FURNITURE
PET PEEVE: BEING LEFT ALONE FOR LONGER THAN FIVE MINUTES

"All knowledge, the totality
of all questions and all answers
is contained in the dog."

FRANZ KAFKA

Top, from left:

BELLE: NAUGHTIEST DEED: ESCAPING
OBSESSION: HUNTING
OWNER: SARA METZGER

HARRY: FAVORITE FOOD: LATTES
NAUGHTIEST DEED: YODELING
OWNERS: CLARENCE AND BECKY JENKINS

Bottom, from left:

FRED: FAVORITE PASTIMES: SLEEPING AND EATING
NAUGHTIEST DEED: OPENING DOORS
OWNER: SARA METZGER

BUCK: OBSESSION: BEING IN ISAAC'S LAP
FAVORITE PASTIME: RIDING IN THE TRUCK WITH ISAAC
OWNER: ISAAC JENKINS

ELLIE: NAUGHTIEST DEED: TERRORIZING THE SHRUBBERY
FAVORITE PASTIME: LAYING IN THE OFFICE ON HOT DAYS
OWNER: SARA METZGER

GEORGIA

FAVORITE FOOD: ANYTHING DEANNA IS COOKING
FAVORITE TOY: ANYTHING THAT MAKES A NOISE
NAUGHTIEST DEED: EATING DEANNA'S GLOVE
OBSESSION: DORI THE HOUSE CAT
FAVORITE PASTIME: PLAYING
OWNER: DEANNA HARRISON
PET PEEVE: BILL HARRISON

MAGGIE

OBSESSION: RABBITS
OWNER: BILL HARRISON
FAVORITE FOOD: TREATS
FAVORITE PASTIME: HUNTING
PET PEEVE: HER SISTER GEORGIA
NAUGHTIEST DEED: DIGGING IN THE BACKYARD
FAVORITE TOY: CHEWING ON HER SISTER GEORGIA

BOXER, 4 | **WM HARRISON WINERY** ST. HELENA, CA

FRANK

OBSESSION: SQUIRRELS
PET PEEVE: HIS SHORT LEGS
OWNERS: NANCY AND JOHN LASSETER
FAVORITE PASTIME: CHECKING SQUIRREL TRAPS
FAVORITE FOOD: ANYTHING THAT HITS THE FLOOR
NAUGHTIEST DEED: DRAGGING AND SHREDDING A SOILED DIAPER THROUGHOUT THE HOUSE

MOOSE

OBSESSION: JACKRABBITS
FAVORITE TOY: SHOOTING WATER
OWNERS: NANCY AND JOHN LASSETER
PET PEEVES: RC CARS, BOATS AND HELICOPTERS
FAVORITE PASTIMES: FISHING AND WATER SPORTS
NAUGHTIEST DEED: CHASING THE CAT TO THE OTHER SIDE OF THE RANCH, RESULTING IN A ONE-MONTH STINT IN THE BARN

NACHA

FAVORITE TOY: TENNIS BALL
OWNERS: JEFF AND MARY STAI
FULL NAME: GARNACHA BLANCA
PET PEEVE: BEING LEFT AT HOME
OBSESSION: TRYING TO BE MOMMA TO KITTENS
FAVORITE PASTIME: GOING ANYWHERE IN THE CAR
NAUGHTIEST DEED: TRYING (UNSUCCESSFULLY) TO LICK THE END OF THE WINE THIEF DURING A BARREL TASTING

MIXED BREED, 9 | **TWISTED OAK WINERY** VALLECITO, CA

ASTI

OWNER: FRED BRANDER
FAVORITE FOOD: CAT FOOD
PET PEEVE: VISITORS WITHOUT PICNICS
OBSESSION: DOGS OUTSIDE HER TRUCK
KNOWN ACCOMPLICES: GWYNNE AND SADIE
FAVORITE PASTIME: KNOWING WHERE FRED IS AT ALL TIMES
NAUGHTIEST DEED: RUNNING THROUGH FRESHLY POURED CONCRETE

GUS

FAVORITE FOOD: FIGS
FAVORITE TOY: MONKEY
OWNERS: JOAN AND STAN BOYD
FAVORITE PASTIME: SWIMMING IN THE RIVER
PET PEEVE: DELIVERY TRUCKS WITHOUT TREATS
NAUGHTIEST DEED: STEALING VISITORS' WATER BOTTLES

BUDDY

FAVORITE TOY: GUS
FAVORITE FOOD: BULLY STICKS
OWNERS: JOAN AND STAN BOYD
NAUGHTIEST DEED: OPENING DOORS
FAVORITE PASTIME: RIDING IN THE CART

JACK

PET PEEVE: BATHS
FAVORITE TOY: RUBBER FROG
FAVORITE PASTIME: SWIMMING IN THE WATER RESERVOIRS
NAUGHTIEST DEED: STEALING A BURNING LOG OUT OF THE FIREPLACE AND RUNNING AROUND THE HOUSE WITH IT
OWNERS: ANTHONY AND SUZANNE TRUCHARD

COOPER

FAVORITE TOY: SQUEAKY PIG
OWNERS: RICHARD AND ALIS ARROWOOD
NAUGHTIEST DEED: OPENING THE PANTRY DOOR TO EAT A WHOLE HUCKLEBERRY PIE
PET PEEVE: PEOPLE LOOKING INTO HIS EYES
OBSESSIONS: POINTING AND CHASING BIRDS
FAVORITE PASTIME: HUNTING FOR GROUSE IN MONTANA
FAVORITE FOOD: ANYTHING COMESTIBLE FROM YOUR POCKET

ROSCO

PET PEEVE: BATH TIME
OWNER: KERRY ARROWOOD
NAUGHTIEST DEED: EATING CAT POOP
FAVORITE FOOD: BEEF JERKY COOKIE TREATS
KNOWN ACCOMPLICE: BEAR THE GREAT PYRENEES
FAVORITE TOY: A VERY LOUD, SQUEAKY RUBBER BALL
FAVORITE PASTIME: RIDING ON A HORSE WITH KERRY

AMERICAN BRITTANY, 4 & FRENCH BULLDOG, 4 | **AMAPOLA CREEK WINERY BY RICHARD ARROWOOD** SONOMA, CA

RALLY

PET PEEVE: BEING COLD
FAVORITE FOOD: TRI-TIP
FAVORITE PASTIME: SKATEBOARDING
OWNERS: KATIE OTA AND JONMIKEL RODRIGUEZ
OBSESSIONS: SNUGGLING AND PLAYING AT THE BEACH
NAUGHTIEST DEED: EATING AN ENTIRE WOODEN DRAGON SCULPTURE
KNOWN ACCOMPLICES: NAHLA THE DOG AND BILL MURRAY THE CAT

ENZO

OWNER: CASEY ZARNES
PET PEEVE: HAVING HIS TOENAILS TRIMMED
OBSESSIONS: TENNIS BALLS AND SQUIRRELS
FAVORITE FOODS: RAW CHICKEN LEGS AND CARROTS
FAVORITE PASTIMES: SWIMMING AND SQUIRREL HUNTING
FAVORITE TOY: ANYTHING THAT CAN BE CHEWED OR THROWN
NAUGHTIEST DEED: PULLING SHEETS OFF A BED TO MAKE A NEST IN HIS DOG BED

GERMAN SHORTHAIRED POINTER X, 4 | **BONNY DOON VINEYARD** DAVENPORT, CA

NINER

FAVORITE TOY: BALL
FAVORITE FOOD: KIBBLE
OWNER: JASON ROBIDEAUX
NAUGHTIEST DEED: CHEWING
OBSESSION: CHASING HIS BALL
FAVORITE PASTIME: PLAYING FETCH
PET PEEVE: NOT BEING ALLOWED ON THE COUCH

HARLEY

OWNERS: MICHELE AND BOB SWENSEN
FAVORITE PASTIME: BEING A 70LB LAP DOG
FAVORITE FOOD: UNCOOKED PASTA NOODLES
PET PEEVE: WALKING ACROSS RAILWAY TRACKS
OBSESSION: GETTING HIS HEAD AND EARS SCRATCHED
NAUGHTIEST DEED: ROLLING IN SOMETHING MUDDY AND STINKY

MOCHA

FAVORITE TOY: ANY SMALL CHILDREN'S TOY THAT WILL FIT INTO HER MOUTH
OWNER: CHERYL MURPHY DURZY
FAVORITE FOOD: ANYTHING FED UNDER THE TABLE BY THE KIDS
FAVORITE PASTIME: SLEEPING
OBSESSION: THE BEACH
PET PEEVE: THE CAR

SULLY

OBSESSION: FRISBEE
PET PEEVE: BEING LEFT BEHIND WHEN JESSICA COMES TO WORK
OWNERS: JESSICA CASE AND JAY ARCHIBALD
FAVORITE PASTIME: SLEEPING ON THE COUCH
FAVORITE FOOD: THANKSGIVING DINNER PAIRED WITH A LITTLE RED WINE

GRIFFIN

FAVORITE PASTIMES: DIGGING FOR GOPHERS AND CHASING KEITH
FAVORITE FOOD: PULLED PORK TACOS WITH CABERNET FRANC
OWNERS: PAM STARR AND NORM LARSEN
NAUGHTIEST DEED: STEALING CHARCUTERIE FROM THE KITCHEN COUNTER
OBSESSION: JUMPING STRAIGHT UP IN THE AIR SO THAT HIS HEAD IS AT THE SAME HEIGHT AS YOURS

KEITH RICHARDS

FAVORITE PASTIME: HANGING OUT WITH THE SILVERADO PICKUPS DURING BAND REHEARSALS
OWNERS: HEIDI AND SHANE SOLDINGER
NAUGHTIEST DEED: NAPPING ON THE JOB
PET PEEVE: EVERY TIME MICK JAGGER RELEASES A SOLO ALBUM
KNOWN ACCOMPLICES: GRIFF, SULLY, KAISER, MICK, RONNIE AND CHARLIE

CROCKER & STARR WINERY ST. HELENA, CA | BOXER, 7, WIREHAIRED POINTING GRIFFON, 5 & MIXED BREED, 3

BOB MARLEY

OWNER: TIM SKOGSTROM
FAVORITE TOY: STUFFED PEACOCK
NAUGHTIEST DEED: SNEAKING INTO THE RESTAURANT AND CLEANING UNDER ALL THE BOOTHS
PET PEEVE: BEING CAUGHT UNDER THE BOOTHS BEFORE HE FINISHES THE JOB
FAVORITE FOOD: WILD TURKEY NECKS
FAVORITE PASTIME: LAYING ON THE RUG IN FRONT OF THE TASTING ROOM AND HAVING HIS BELLY RUBBED

GENNA ROSE

OBSESSION: PEOPLE'S FEET
FAVORITE TOY: DRESS HEMLINES
FAVORITE FOOD: COSTCO DOG TREATS
PET PEEVE: NOT BEING PLAYED WITH
NAUGHTIEST DEED: POOING BEHIND THE WINE BARRELS IN THE TASTING ROOM
FAVORITE PASTIME: CHASING THE SEVEN-YEAR-OLD GERMAN SHEPHERD
OWNERS: JIM AND MARIBETH JACOBSEN

VITO

OBSESSION: TENNIS BALLS
PET PEEVES: CATS AND ZEKE
NAUGHTIEST DEED: SWALLOWING HALF A BLACK WALNUT SHELL
FAVORITE TOY: TICKLE THE BOSTON
OWNERS: RAY AND LORI TELDESCHI
FAVORITE PASTIME: BLOWING BULLDOG SNOT ON LORI'S CLEAN WINDOWS
FAVORITE FOODS: POPCORN AND BANANAS

ZEKE

OBSESSION: RAY
OWNERS: RAY AND LORI TELDESCHI
FAVORITE TOY: ANYTHING HE CAN BURY
PET PEEVE: WYATT THE SPRINGER SPANIEL
FAVORITE FOODS: BBQ CHICKEN AND SMOKED FISH
FAVORITE PASTIME: CHASING RABBITS IN THE VINEYARD
NAUGHTIEST DEEDS: DESTROYING NUMEROUS PHONE BOOKS AND TAKING SMOKED FISH OUT OF THE FRIDGE

TICKLE

OBSESSION: TOYS
FAVORITE FOOD: LIVER
PET PEEVE: THE VACUUM CLEANER
OWNERS: RAY AND LORI TELDESCHI
FAVORITE TOY: ANYTHING WITH STUFFING
FAVORITE PASTIMES: SNUGGLING AND GETTING BELLY RUBS
NAUGHTIEST DEED: PLAYING 'CATCH ME IF YOU CAN' WHEN IT'S TIME TO GO

JACK DANIEL

OWNER: DARCI HILL
FAVORITE TOY: LANDON
FAVORITE PASTIME: EATING
PET PEEVES: CHARLOTTE AND LANDON
FAVORITE FOOD: TRADER JOE'S LEMON BARS
NAUGHTIEST DEED: PEEING IN THE LOUNGEROOM
OBSESSION: CHASING CROWS WHEN THEY LAND ON THE WATER FOUNTAIN

ROVER, BORDEAUX COLLIE

by Lori Crantford

IF YOU'VE BEEN LUCKY ENOUGH to find yourself deep in the heart of California wine country, even if just for a day, then you've heard the legend. Of a dog. A dog of unparalleled intelligence, unrivaled good looks, and ball-licking skills the envy of every canine and pro wrestler west of the Mississippi.

Well, the legend's true. I'm Rover, Bordeaux Collie. And here's my story.

My people were originally East Coast folks. You know, Central Barkers. Sure there were lots of advantages to that life: gourmet doggie bags and pedigreed bitches as far as the eye could see. A city where anything is possible. Where else could a Golden Retriever learn to talk, walk upright, comb his hair over and call himself Donald Trump?

By the time I came around, my people had plenty of fine wine experience. (Oh come on. Yes, dogs drink wine. I Shih Tzu not. Ever get that sneaking feeling every time you left your wine glass unattended at a party, that when you returned it was less full than you remembered? That was us. My Aunt Vi – or Viognier if you know what's good for you – holds the record for party tastings. For a Corgi, that girl can hold her liquor. Their secret? Low center of gravity. Oh, and drinking out of the toilet? Strictly palate cleansing.)

Party tastings weren't enough for me, however. I needed to be where the action was, where it all started. Wasn't I all about soil? Wasn't I all about tannins? You know, those little things that explode during the holidays? The one with the song: *O Tannin Bombs*. Wasn't I just like a great wine, excellent from nose to finish? Yes. I. Was.

With California as my destination, I set out on a cross-country trek that would make Lassie look like a pussy ... cat. I encountered every kind of terrain, every kind of weather, every kind of creature known and unknown to man. And that was just in Jersey.

In Kentucky I met a drop-dead gorgeous Cocker Spaniel named Red – I think she was a blend – who was sweet-tempered until she threw back a few distilled peaches. You know, some fruits are meant to be drunk, and others are just meant to be served over ice-cream.

By the time I made Oklahoma, I was beginning to appreciate those wide-open spaces.

There was something appealing about those never-ending skies, that tumbleweed tundra. For a couple of days, I considered staying there, being at home, home on the range. "Range Rover." It had a nice ring to it.

But I pushed onward to my goal. In LA I met a flirty but flighty little Miniature Poodle with whom I whiled away a memorable evening. As they all do, she begged me to stay, but I don't roll over for beggars. In wine terminology, we'd call her a real corker, which is to say she had a screwcap loose.

With steely determination, I miraculously made my way straight through San Francisco, across the great Golden Gate Bridge – which has been marked big time, my friend, so don't even think about it – and up into God's country, which we all know, if you listen to it backwards, is Dog's country.

Now I live where I was born to live, and my cross-country journey is the stuff of legends. I patrol the fields, keep watch over the grapes, and judging by the "Oh my!" and "I never!" and "If I could do that I wouldn't have gotten married!" phrases that are uttered by our winery customers, I know that my ball-licking skills are only adding to business.

When you come visit, make sure to taste the Red Rover Reserve. It pairs well with nuts.

LORI CRANTFORD IS AN EMMY-AWARD WINNING WRITER LIVING IN INDIANAPOLIS, INDIANA. SHE IS THE HAPPY OWNER OF TWO CATS AND SEVERAL DOG-EARED BOOKS. DOGS OF SEVERAL FRIENDS (AS WELL AS A FAIR AMOUNT OF THEIR WINE) SERVED AS INSPIRATION FOR THIS STORY. THIS STORY HAS BEEN REPRINTED FROM *WINE DOGS USA 2*, PUBLISHED 2008.

MAGGIE

OWNERS: JENNIFER AND HERB LAMB
FAVORITE FOOD: RIPE PEACHES RIGHT OFF THE TREE
NAUGHTIEST DEED: CHASING AND EATING CHICKENS
PET PEEVE: CAMO WHEN SHE WANTS TO PLAY ROUGH
OBSESSION: COMING INSIDE WHEN THE WEATHER'S COLD
KNOWN ACCOMPLICE: CHLOE, THE 16-YEAR-OLD TABBY CAT
FAVORITE PASTIME: BARKING IN THE VINEYARDS ALL NIGHT LONG

CAMO

OWNERS: JENNIFER AND HERB LAMB
FAVORITE TOY: A SLOBBERY TENNIS BALL
FAVORITE FOOD: WHATEVER IS IN HER DINNER BOWL
FAVORITE PASTIME: PLAYING CATCH WITH A PINE CONE
PET PEEVE: AN EMPTY WATER BOWL AFTER A GAME OF CATCH
NAUGHTIEST DEED: CHEWING ALL THE STUFFING OUT OF HER BED

UVA

PET PEEVE: THE ATV
OBSESSION: THE ATV
KNOWN ACCOMPLICE: PHOEBE
FAVORITE TOYS: FRISBEES AND PHOEBE
OWNERS: MICHELLE AND SHERMAN THACHER
FAVORITE PASTIME: PLAYING WITH SAMMY THE CAT

PHOEBE

FAVORITE FOOD: PICNICS
PET PEEVE: SAMMY THE CAT
KNOWN ACCOMPLICE: UVA AND ABBI
NAUGHTIEST DEED: EATING A PEACOCK
OBSESSION: GOING ON RUNS WITH MICHELLE
OWNERS: MICHELLE AND SHERMAN THACHER
FAVORITE PASTIME: SLEEPING ON COLD FLOORS

COWGIRL KATE

PET PEEVE: THE ROOSTER
FAVORITE FOOD: CHEESE
OWNERS: STEVE AND SUSAN BECKMEN
OBSESSIONS: SQUIRRELS AND ROOSTERS
KNOWN ACCOMPLICES: OTIS AND ICHI THE PIGLET
FAVORITE PASTIMES: CHASING SQUIRRELS AND LONG-DISTANCE BARKING
NAUGHTIEST DEEDS: ATTACKING THE ROOSTER AND ROLLING IN DEAD ANIMALS

OTIS

FAVORITE TOY: SQUEAKY COW
FAVORITE PASTIME: SWIMMING
OWNERS: STEVE AND SUSAN BECKMEN
OBSESSION: CHASING GROUND SQUIRRELS
FAVORITE FOOD: ANYTHING HE CAN FIND, HE'S A LAB!
KNOWN ACCOMPLICES: SUSAN, JASPER, RUTH AND STEVE
NAUGHTIEST DEED: STEALING EGGS FROM THE CHICKEN COOP

LABRADOR, 2 | **BECKMEN VINEYARDS** LOS OLIVOS, CA

D-OG

OWNER: KYLE KNAPP
PET PEEVE: PEOPLE FIGHTING
FAVORITE FOOD: RAW ALMONDS
OBSESSIONS: FRISBEES AND KYLE
FAVORITE PASTIME: GOING TO THE BEACH
KNOWN ACCOMPLICES: SAVANNA AND MILO KNAPP
NAUGHTIEST DEED: GUARDING KYLE'S CLOTHES AND SANDALS

KIEFER

OWNER: MATTHEW GASCO
OBSESSION: SITTING IN THE FRONT SEAT
NAUGHTIEST DEED: BEGGING FOR TREATS
FAVORITE FOODS: SALMON AND COOKIES
PET PEEVES: SMOOTH WOODEN FLOORS AND PEOPLE THAT DON'T BUY AUGUST BRIGGS WINE
KNOWN ACCOMPLICE: CALVIN THE WEIMARANER
FAVORITE PASTIME: MORNING WALKS ON THE TRAIL

DIDIER

FAVORITE FOOD: PIZZA
PET PEEVE: TALL MEN
OWNER: MORGAN CLENDENEN
FAVORITE PASTIMES: TRYING TO BITE THE UPS GUY AND PLAYING WITH CORKS
NAUGHTIEST DEED: TRASH CAN DIVING
OBSESSIONS: THE VACUUM CLEANER AND BITING THE UPS GUY

CHARLIE

OWNER: JIM STOLLBERG
OBSESSION: LICKING TO SAY HELLO
PET PEEVE: ANY BIRD CIRCLING OVERHEAD
NAUGHTIEST DEED: USING HIS GREY HAIR AND WHIMPERING TO GET A TREAT
FAVORITE FOOD: ANYTHING FROM THE BBQ PIT
FAVORITE TOY: ANY VINEYARD ROCK OR STICK
FAVORITE PASTIME: CHASING SQUIRRELS AND BIRDS

ROY

OBSESSION: CHEESE
OWNER: LAURA BOORAS
FAVORITE TOY: HIS BUNNY
PET PEEVE: ANYONE TOUCHING HIS TAIL
FAVORITE PASTIMES: CHEWING TENNIS BALLS AND GREETING EVERYONE AT RIVERBENCH
FAVORITE FOODS: CHEESE, BEER AND CHICKEN
NAUGHTIEST DEED: CHEWING THE OCCASIONAL CORK

RIDGEBACK X, 13 & ENGLISH BULLDOG, 9 | **RIVERBENCH VINEYARD AND WINERY** SANTA MARIA, CA

ARRIE

FAVORITE FOOD: BACON
FAVORITE TOY: RED BALL
OWNERS: NORM AND JENI PRUSA
OBSESSIONS: RED BALL AND NORM
PET PEEVE: LOUD NOISES WHILE SLEEPING
FAVORITE PASTIME: CHASING THE RED BALL

KARMA

FAVORITE TOY: ARRIE
FAVORITE FOOD: BACON
OBSESSION: CHASING BUNNIES
FAVORITE PASTIME: NAPPING
OWNERS: NORM AND JENI PRUSA
NAUGHTIEST DEED: GOING ON LONG UNSUPERVISED ADVENTURES

PET PEEVE: CATS
FAVORITE FOOD: GREENIES
OBSESSION: SLEEPING ON THE BED
FAVORITE TOYS: FOXY AND HEDGEHOG
OWNERS: ELLIE PRICE AND CHRIS TOWT
NAUGHTIEST DEED: EATING THE CAT FOOD
KNOWN ACCOMPLICES: ARRIE AND KARMA
FAVORITE PASTIME: CHASING BUTTERFLIES
MILES

SCOTCH

FAVORITE TOY: MR SQUIRREL
OWNER: BENJAMIN FLAJNIK
OBSESSIONS: KITES, CATS AND MICE
PET PEEVE: SOMEONE WALKING INTO HIS SUNLIGHT WHILE HE'S SUNBATHING
FAVORITE PASTIME: GOPHER HUNTING
FAVORITE FOODS: CHICKEN OR FILET MIGNON
NAUGHTIEST DEED: DIGGING HOLES IN THE BACKYARD

SPOT

OWNER: CLEMENTINE BERLIN
OBSESSION: GETTING ALL THE ATTENTION
NAUGHTIEST DEED: SHAMELESSLY STEALING ALL GUESTS' ATTENTION FOR HIMSELF
KNOWN ACCOMPLICE: HIS BROTHER, INKY
FAVORITE FOOD: KIBBLE WITH HOT CHICKEN BROTH

INKY

OWNER: BEATRICE BERLIN
KNOWN ACCOMPLICE: HIS BROTHER, SPOT
NAUGHTIEST DEED: MUD-AND-BLOOD-SPECKLED DRAMA
FAVORITE PASTIME: SNUGGLING UNDER BEATRICE'S COVERS
FAVORITE FOOD: FREEZE-DRIED LIVER WITH EL MOLINO PINOT

MAGGIE

OWNER: JOHN IBACH
PET PEEVE: HER COLLAR
FAVORITE PASTIME: HOWLING TO MUSIC
FAVORITE TOY: SQUEAKY ROPE ANIMAL
OBSESSION: BURROWING UNDER COVERS
KNOWN ACCOMPLICES: PENNY AND THANG
NAUGHTIEST DEED: TORMENTING HER BROTHER

HANNA

OWNER: PAUL WARSON
FAVORITE FOOD: ANYTHING STOLEN
FAVORITE PASTIME: STEALING FOOD
FAVORITE TOY: ANYTHING SHE CAN SLOWLY RIP APART
OBSESSIONS: THE LITTER BOX AND WALKING HER TRAILS
KNOWN ACCOMPLICES: HER PUG BARNEY AND HER CAT DK
PET PEEVE: NOT GETTING HER SCRATCHES FOR LONG ENOUGH
NAUGHTIEST DEED: JUMPING ONTO A TABLE AND EATING A BREAKFAST BUFFET

MARGARITA

OBSESSION: BRIAN
OWNER: BRIAN KOSI
PET PEEVE: HOT AIR BALLOONS
FAVORITE FOOD: BONE-IN RIB-EYE STEAKS
KNOWN ACCOMPLICE: BONNIE THE BLACK CAT
FAVORITE TOY: HER STUFFED TEDDY BEAR OF THE WEEK
FAVORITE PASTIMES: CAMPING AND BACKPACKING IN THE HIGH SIERRAS
NAUGHTIEST DEED: CHEWING THROUGH A FENCE TO GET AWAY FROM HOT AIR BALLOONS

FREEMARK ABBEY WINERY ST. HELENA, CA | LABRADOR X, 11

MURRAY

PET PEEVE: BEING ALONE
FAVORITE FOOD: DICK VAN PATTEN'S "SPECIAL DINNER"
OWNER: MICHAEL LANCASTER
OBSESSIONS: FOOD AND HOCKEY ON ESPN
NAUGHTIEST DEED: NOT FIT FOR PUBLICATION
FAVORITE PASTIME: HIDING TOYS IN THE BACKYARD

CALI

OWNER: SARAH RAPPENSPERGER
FAVORITE FOOD: 3 DOG BAKERY PEANUT BUTTER COOKIES
FAVORITE TOY: SQUEAKY REINDEER
OBSESSION: SNIFFING OUT GOPHERS
NAUGHTIEST DEED: EATING SARAH'S SOCKS
PET PEEVE: GETTING HIS TEETH BRUSHED
FAVORITE PASTIME: RUNNING AT THE DOG PARK

AJAX

FAVORITE TOY: STICKS
PET PEEVE: BEING BORED
FAVORITE PASTIMES: LONG WALKS AND EXPLORATIONS
OBSESSION: WALKS, WALKS, WALKS AND MORE WALKS
OWNER: MICHAEL LANCASTER
NAUGHTIEST DEED: TALKING TO STRANGERS

AUSTRALIAN SHEPHERD X, 9, FOXHOUND X, 2 & BORDER COLLIE, 8 | **TIN BARN VINEYARDS** SONOMA, CA

STEVE

OWNER: KEVIN MILLS
NAUGHTIEST DEED: EATING THE PRIUS
FAVORITE FOODS: STEAK, WALNUTS AND EGGS
PET PEEVES: BEING LEFT BEHIND AND SAILING
OBSESSIONS: KEVIN AND RED GRAPES ONCE THEY REACH 22 BRIX
FAVORITE PASTIME: HELPING THE WINEMAKER MAKE PICKING DECISIONS

SULA

OWNER: AARON PIOTTER
PET PEEVE: BEING SNUCK UP ON
OBSESSION: JUMPING ONTO LAPS
KNOWN ACCOMPLICES: MACY AND BODIE (WHO LIVE IN CHARLES SCHULZ'S ORIGINAL HOUSE)
FAVORITE TOY: STUFFED MINI MALLARD DUCK
FAVORITE PASTIME: WALKING ON HER HIND LEGS

PATTERDALE TERRIER, 2 | **FERRARI-CARANO VINEYARDS AND WINERY** HEALDSBURG, CA

"From the dog's point of view,
his master is an elongated
and abnormally cunning dog."

MABEL LOUISE ROBINSON

CHARLIE

OWNER: BREANNA TAMBURIN
FAVORITE TOY: LITTLE STUFFED BUNNY
PET PEEVE: HAVING HER PAWS TOUCHED
FAVORITE PASTIMES: PLAYING TUG-OF-WAR WITH ROSCOE AND CHASING AFTER LEAVES
OBSESSIONS: PEOPLE, FOOD AND BELLY RUBS
NAUGHTIEST DEED: SNEAKING INTO THE GARBAGE
FAVORITE FOODS: SALMON, CHICKEN AND SPAGHETTI

PADDY

OBSESSION: LICKING
OWNER: MARK DAVIS
FAVORITE TOY: GORDY THE STUFFED MOOSE
FAVORITE PASTIMES: LOUNGING ON THE COUCH AND RUNNING IN THE DRY CREEKBED
FAVORITE FOODS: SEARED SCALLOPS WITH A LIGHT TRUFFLE SAUCE AND KIBBLE
NAUGHTIEST DEED: HAVING AN ACCIDENT (OF THE 2ND KIND) IN THE BACK OF THE CAR
PET PEEVES: PEOPLE THINKING HIS NAME IS PATTY AND THE GANG OF LOCAL CHIHUAHUAS

O'BRIEN ESTATE WINERY NAPA, CA | AMERICAN STAFFORDSHIRE TERRIER X, 6 MONTHS

JAKE

PET PEEVE: STRANGERS
FAVORITE FOODS: TURKEY AND KIBBLE
OWNERS: MARCELLA AND FESS PARKER
KNOWN ACCOMPLICES: LUCY AND MARCELLA
NAUGHTIEST DEED: RAIDING THE WASTE BASKET

FESS PARKER

BREED: TEXAN
FAVORITE PASTIME: ADMIRING ATTRACTIVE LADIES
FAVORITE FOOD: THE PARKER BURGER
FAVORITE TOY: 99 HUMMER
NAUGHTIEST DEED: KISSING PATRICIA BRADBURY WHEN HE WAS THREE
PET PEEVE: TRANSPARENT POLITICIANS
KNOWN ACCOMPLICE: MARCELLA

LUCY

PET PEEVE: STRANGERS
FAVORITE PASTIME: SLEEPING
FAVORITE FOOD: COTTAGE CHEESE
KNOWN ACCOMPLICES: JAKE AND FESS
OWNERS: MARCELLA AND FESS PARKER

SPARTICUS

PET PEEVE: HATS
OBSESSION: FETCHING BARREL BUNGS
NAUGHTIEST DEED: BEING A 80-LB LAP DOG
OWNER: STEPHEN KROENER
FAVORITE FOOD: GUESTS' TREATS
FAVORITE TOYS: BARREL BUNGS AND A SMALL RUBBER CART WHEEL

ASHA

OBSESSION: HUMANS
FAVORITE TOY: ANYTHING THAT SPARTICUS HAS
OWNER: STEPHEN KROENER
FAVORITE PASTIME: LAYING AROUND AND STARING AT YOU THROUGH A WINDOW
NAUGHTIEST DEED: CHEWING HOLES IN WOODEN FENCES

PENNY

FAVORITE TOY: ZORRO
NAUGHTIEST DEED: HIGH-PITCHED BARKING
PET PEEVE: BELLY RUBS THAT AREN'T LONG ENOUGH
OWNER: STEPHEN KROENER
FAVORITE PASTIME: ROLLING OVER FOR A BELLY RUB FROM TASTING ROOM GUESTS

DOGS MAKE A HOME OUT OF A WINERY

by Eve Bushman

PICTURE THE IDEAL WINERY TASTING ROOM and the mind conjures up a wooden bar, a pour out bucket, a cash register, a couple of dusty gold or silver ribbons adorning bottles on display, and a lone wine-tender waiting for you to review his daily tasting selections.

Now add a dog and the image changes. The tasting room now has a lit fireplace framed by sofas and overstuffed pillows, a middle-aged couple behind the bar, country music, framed photos of the grounds and several more of the winery family. In the corner is a dog's bed, lined in fleece, and hanging off one edge: a rope pull toy just itching for you to pick it up and see if a dog comes running in to grab the other end, engaging you in a long friendly battle.

You may mosey up to the inviting tasting bar, and within moments a cold wet nose tickles you behind the knees.

You will possibly take your glass outside onto a porch bathed in sunlight, lingering over a Paso Robles Rhône blend or Zinfandel; you know that the dog is following as you hear the light tap of toenails rhythmically hitting the oak flooring. You now notice a water dish under a spout and think, dang, maybe I could have brought my dog with me.

No bark, no bite, and you've found a welcoming winery that knows the power of a winery dog.

So why do dogs matter in a winery? They matter just like they belong in any family – they become an extension of their winemaker. Think about it this way: man's best friend is also a great conversation starter.

"Hello mate, nice winery you have here..." kind of trails off if the guest is new to wines, new to the winery, only drinks whites, only drinks reds, in a hurry to get to the next winery, on a mission to drink everything, looks nervous, or ... is completely out of their element.

In struts Sammy the smiling German Shepherd or Willie the wildly active Welsh Corgi to get that visitor ... a little more relaxed. The visitor interacts with the winery pooch and it feels like they're more a part of the winery. A tickle under the chin paired with a little winery intro, a scratch behind the ear for that first sip, and a full pat down the length of the pup's silky back with the final pour.

And I've had it happen to me. I walked smack dab into a *Wine Dogs* photo shoot at Silver Horse Winery in Paso Robles just last year. I ended up at the winery much longer than I had planned.

In writing this story, I called the winery for an update on the dogs. I'm happy to report that all four Labradors, the two males Sparticus and Zorro, and two females Asha and Penny, are all still living amongst the vines.

Every night, when the tasting room closes, two go home with the winemaker and the other two go home with the family. Seventy-five percent of the time, there will be one of the four cozying up the tasting room.

As the Labs are on "the loose" they may lend their warmth to a wedding in the grounds, but due to this, I'm told, they have all grown overweight – to the point where guests must now refrain from sharing their treats! One other tidbit of news to report, the Labs seem to enjoy howling nightly – along with the coyotes.

If you take a trip to Silver Horse there are two items, that aren't wine, which you might be lucky enough to find in the tasting room. One is the last edition of *Wine Dogs USA* that I'm told "flew out the door and sold out", the other is a handcrafted dog bed using barrel staves and comfy pads. Apparently, the Labs love their new beds.

So, backing up a bit to my original thought, besides hanging with the Labs at Silver Horse in Paso, I want to contemplate the richness of life over my Stags Leap Napa Cabernet, pair a warm day in Santa Ynez with a Chardonnay in a glass covered in condensation and a breezy late afternoon in Sonoma with a Pinot Noir full of bright cherry flavor.

And in each scenario, there is a furry friendly dog in my minds-eye. Seated, with one paw stretched over one of my feet – keeping me warm, cozy and still while I savor the moment, and the wine. And every time he looks up at me, and opens his mouth just to breathe, Mother Nature rewards me with that built-in smile. Now that's what I call a pairing.

At times, people have been known to make an emotional buy at a winery because of the experience they had in the tasting room. Charmed by the hosts, the wine, the scenery or the family pet. The wine, of course, is the focal point, the center framed by the winery.

But when that wine buyer gets home, and the memory of a tasting bar or a friendly winemaker doesn't suffice, having that wine glass in one hand, and your own pup's paw in the other, will.

So what's the real difference in adding the pup to the tasting room experience? The winery feels more like home, and a place you will be itching to return to just like a tug o' war with a rope pull.

Still not sure? Many Paso Robles wineries would have to disagree as they annually support a fundraiser, aptly named *Wine 4 Paws*. Napa Valley vintners support their own annual event, *Canine Heroes Wine Auction*. And, not to leave others out, there is *Canines Uncorked* in Oregon, *Hair of the Dog* in Massachusetts, *Woof and Wine* in New York, *Wags, Whiskers and Wine* in Delaware, *Every Dog Counts* in Indiana, the *Poochapalooza* in Washington ... and the sole beneficiary of all of that wonderful wine tasting is: our dogs.

EVE BUSHMAN, A WINE/SPIRITS/LIFESTYLE WRITER, HOSTS AND MARKETS WINE EVENTS FOR NON-PROFITS AND FOR-PROFITS, AS WELL AS HER OWN EVE WINE 101 EVENTS. SHE PROMOTES THE WINE INDUSTRY WITH SOCIAL NETWORKING AND DAILY CONTENT ON HER WEBSITE. IN 2012 EVE CREATED EVE'S WINE 101 CONSULTING WITH HER BUSINESS PARTNER MICHAEL PERLIS. HER WINE COLUMNS CAN BE FOUND AT EVEWINE101.COM, SCVELITEMAGAZINE.COM AND SCVBEACON.COM HER OWN WINE DOG, A WELSH CORGI NAMED TYSON, IS TASKED WITH THE JOB OF BARKING AT HER WHEN SHE ATTEMPTS TO UNLOCK HER CELLAR WITHOUT HER HUSBAND PRESENT.
THIS STORY HAS BEEN REPRINTED FROM *WINE DOGS USA 3*, PUBLISHED 2012.

ZORRO

FAVORITE TOY: PENNY
OWNER: STEPHEN KROENER
NAUGHTIEST DEED: ESCAPING
PET PEEVE: NOT BEING ABLE TO GET INTO THE BACK OF THE TRUCK FOR ADVENTURES
OBSESSION: CHASING ANYTHING ON WHEELS
KNOWN ACCOMPLICES: ASHA, SPARTICUS AND PENNY

LABRADOR, 8 | **SILVER HORSE WINERY** SAN MIGUEL, CA

HENRY

OWNER: JOHN TEVIS
PET PEEVE: PRETENTIOUS WINE SNOBS
FAVORITE FOODS: TRI-TIP AND BURRITOS
FAVORITE TOY: STUFFED CHRISTMAS TREE PILLOW
FAVORITE PASTIMES: GOING TO THE BEACH AND HIKING
NAUGHTIEST DEED: STEALING AND EATING JOHN'S BURRITO
OBSESSION: WOMEN'S PURSES (A POSSIBLE SOURCE OF TREATS)

RAMONE

FAVORITE PASTIME: NAPPING ON HIS BACK WITH ALL FOUR LEGS IN THE AIR
OWNERS: MICHAEL, TERRI AND SOPHIA TRUJILLO
KNOWN ACCOMPLICE: DARLA, HIS ONE TRUE LOVE
FAVORITE TOY: AN ANNOYING HONKING HEDGEHOG
PET PEEVE: NOT BEING ALLOWED AT THE DINNER TABLE
NAUGHTIEST DEED: LICKING SUNSCREEN OFF PEOPLE'S FACES

COOPER

PET PEEVE: RATTLESNAKES
OWNERS: KERRY AND TOM EDDY
KNOWN ACCOMPLICE: PIPER THE CAT
FAVORITE FOOD: ANYTHING WITH MEAT
FAVORITE PASTIME: WATCHING THE SUNSET
OBSESSION: SNIFFING OUT BAD GUY RODENTS
NAUGHTIEST DEED: BEGGING FOR DINNER SCRAPS

FINN

OWNER: MICHAEL UYTENGSU
FAVORITE TOY: THE FOUNTAIN AT THE WINERY
OBSESSIONS: SWIMMING AND SCENT TRACKING
NAUGHTIEST DEED: SNEAKING OUT OF THE HOUSE IN THE MIDDLE OF THE NIGHT TO GO SWIMMING
FAVORITE FOODS: BISON, GOURMET CHEESE AND TRUFFLES
FAVORITE PASTIMES: TRUFFLE HUNTING AND AGILITY CLASSES
PET PEEVE: NOT BEING ALLOWED IN THE POOL AT THE POLO CLUB

LAGOTTO ROMAGNOLO, 3 | **TUSK ESTATES** OAKVILLE, CA

ELVIS

OWNER: DANIEL SANTA
FAVORITE TOY: TENNIS BALL
FAVORITE PASTIME: PLAYING FETCH
OBSESSION: GARY THE HOT DOG VENDOR
FAVORITE FOODS: HAPPY HIPS DOG FOOD AND HOT DOGS
PET PEEVES: SKATEBOARDS AND DOGS SNIFFING HIS BUTT
NAUGHTIEST DEED: TAKING A DUMP IN DANIEL'S SHOE WHEN LEFT BEHIND

KENAI

OBSESSION: BALLS
FAVORITE TOY: BALLS
PET PEEVE: RELAXING
FAVORITE FOOD: CHEESE
OWNER: JACKIE MEISINGER
FAVORITE PASTIME: BALL CHASING
NAUGHTIEST DEED: EATING JACKIE'S DESIGNER SHOES

CHELSEA

FAVORITE TOY: HER MOM, SOHO
PET PEEVE: BEING LEFT AT HOME ALONE
OWNERS: CLAY AND CARRIE MAURITSON
FAVORITE PASTIME: POSING FOR PHOTOS
OBSESSION: ESCAPING FROM THE TASTING ROOM
NAUGHTIEST DEED: ESCAPING FROM THE TASTING ROOM

SOHO

FAVORITE TOY: BARREL BUNGS
OBSESSION: CLAY, HER OWNER
PET PEEVE: CHILDREN PULLING HER TAIL
OWNERS: CLAY AND CARRIE MAURITSON
FAVORITE PASTIME: GREETING CUSTOMERS
KNOWN ACCOMPLICE: HER DAUGHTER, CHELSEA
NAUGHTIEST DEED: CHASING RABBITS IN THE VINEYARDS

OWNERS: AMY AND PAUL KEMP
FAVORITE PASTIME: USING HIS BIG BROWN EYES TO CONVINCE WINERY VISITORS THAT HE IS STARVING
PET PEEVE: NOT GETTING THE ATTENTION HE DESERVES
KNOWN ACCOMPLICE: THE NORCAL GSP RESCUE ORGANIZATION
NAUGHTIEST DEED: CATCHING A BIG CROW AND DROPPING IT AT AMY'S FEET

MO

RUBY

PET PEEVE: YELLING
OWNERS: RENAE AND BRUCE PERRY
NAUGHTIEST DEED: EATING 15 BAGELS AND HIDING THE REST IN THE FURNITURE
OBSESSIONS: RENAE AND TENNIS BALLS
KNOWN ACCOMPLICES: BUFFY AND ROOTY FROM KOKOMO
FAVORITE PASTIME: CHASING TENNIS BALLS IN THE VINEYARD

HAROLD'S DOG

by Cole Danehower

HAROLD DID NOT LIKE DOGS; he hadn't liked them – so he said – since one bit him when he was an infant. If the subject came up, he'd show you a barely perceptible scratch (he called it a scar) just above his right elbow. "Damn cur took out two inches of skin," he'd say.

In fact, animals in general didn't appeal to Harold, and some in particular caused him real trouble. He attributed the breakup of his marriage to his allergy to cats, he fought incessant battles against "those vile moles" in the vineyard, "cursed pesky" birds at harvest time, and in recent years, a few "vicious black bear brutes" that ravaged the vines at the edges of what he considered to be "his" vineyard.

Of course, Harold didn't much like people, either. He lived alone in a small old house at the far end of a 35-acre vineyard, hard up against the stony foothills of a boundary mountain in Southern Oregon. It was about as distant from the tasting room of the winery that employed him as it was possible to get and still be on the owner's land. Unfortunately, though, it was also closer to the bears, moles, and birds.

What Harold did like was grapevines, and he had a way with them. He'd fallen into the vineyard business seventeen years ago when a local farmer hired him to tend a newly planted vineyard. They both figured that fruit was fruit, and since Harold already knew all about peach orchards he could figure out how to grow good grapes. Implausibly, they were right.

As the vintages went by, Harold grew closer and closer to his grapes. He somehow seemed in touch with the rhythms of the vines and the earth, and the winemakers who purchased the fruit complimented him and the owner, and told the owner that he could never let Harold go because nobody else could grow grapes as good as he could.

For Harold, it had been a satisfying career. He got paid to work among the vines he loved, and he could live his solitary life comfortably insulated from the people he loathed. Even when the old farmer sold the vineyard to an absentee couple from Northern California, who built a small but fancy winery and what they called a "visitor facility", Harold's life continued as before: they enthusiastically maintained Harold's employment, only asking that he also be caretaker of the new building.

Of course, there were still the moles and birds and bears to plague him, but at least the new owners had hired a bright young woman to run the sales side of the winery so Harold didn't have to deal with the people that increasingly were visiting the new winery.

One early spring morning, when Harold was walking through the vineyard to go and unlock the tasting room before business hours began, he was unpleasantly brought to a sudden stop. Standing there in front of him between the vine rows was a dog.

"Shoo!" he shouted. "Get on. Go! Get away."

He didn't know what kind of dog it was. It had a long butterscotch-colored coat and a gangly pink tongue that dangled off the side of his mouth, pulsing with the dog's breath and threatening to get caught up in the jangle of sharp white teeth that showed so clearly.

The more Harold shouted at the dog, the faster it seemed the dog's tail wagged. When Harold tried lunging toward it threateningly, the dog just jumped back and wagged more fiercely.

By the time Harold got up to the winery, he had realized he wouldn't be able to shake the dog – it just followed behind him, at a safe distance. Harold thought about throwing a rock at it, but decided if he ended up hurting the dog it would just lie there yelping, and then he'd have to do something about it, so he decided to just ignore it.

When the tasting room woman came in that day, she went right over to the dog and petted it, got it a dish of fresh water, and found some old crackers to feed it. The next day, things pretty much repeated itself. And the next. And many more following that.

Weeks went by; vine leaves unfolded, grape flowers bloomed, and clusters began to swell. A shiny water bowl and painted dog dish appeared on the tasting room patio, a couple of old straw bales were made into a makeshift dog house on the building's side, and visitors billed and cooed around the dog as they sat and sipped their wine samples.

This was all fine with Harold. Except for meeting up with the dog in the vine rows each morning, he had no interaction with it. He never saw it during the daytime or at night, he knew it had acquired a name, but he refused to remember it, it never asked him for attention or affection, and Harold ignored the dog when he saw it in the vineyard – it had become a background feature of the landscape to Harold.

That all changed late one evening about three weeks after veraison. The cool air from the top of the mountain behind the vineyard had begun slumping down across the grape rows, lightly chilling the warmth of the day. The sun was well behind more distant hills and the sky was turning a vibrant cobalt blue.

Harold was finishing an inspection of the vines when he heard what sounded like the noise of crashing underbrush coming from the near end of the vineyard, over toward his house. It was not a noise he had heard before, and curious, he began walking toward it. And then running.

There was suddenly the sound of barking and growling all at once, and thrashing noises of violence. Harold thought about ducking into the house to get his gun, but realized it was back in the closet, unloaded, and would be of little help in the immediacy of the ruckus.

Running, he turned the end of a vine row and suddenly stopped. Three rows down, just at the end, were two black bears being held at bay by the yelping, howling, barking dog. The dog's tail was sharp in the air, the fur stood up on its back, its feet were widely planted, and it was barking in a machine-gun rhythm.

Harold was transfixed. The slow and eager vineyard dog that so loved being petted by tasting room patrons was now a banshee virtually attacking two bears who were intent on getting nearly ripe grapes from Harold's vines. The mangy thing was saving his grapes!

Suddenly one of the bears took a fast step toward the dog, testing its defense of the vines. The dog launched itself at the bear, rising off the ground and sinking its teeth into the furry flesh just above its right leg. The bear let out a scream and whirled around with its other leg, firmly smacking the dog dead on its side, sending it flying some feet before it crashed into the dirt while Harold stared on.

But the dog's attack had been enough for the bears. With a lumbering gait and a reluctant growl, they each turned back toward the underbrush and retreated to the rocky face of the foothills.

Harold rushed to the dog's side. It lay still. He could see no marks, but it was lifeless. Yet it couldn't be dead. It couldn't be ... not after having saved Harold's grapes ...

Suddenly Harold remembered playing football as a kid. He recalled being hit by a big linebacker. He remembered lying dazed on the ground, puzzled and panicked at having the breath knocked out of him.

That was it! The dog's breath had been knocked out of it by the bear's punch. The dog had to get it back. Without thinking, Harold kicked the dog in the chest – not too hard. That was it! That was the shock the dog needed. Suddenly its mouth shot open and its tongue started pulsing and it grunted and gasped for breath. It was back. It was breathing.

Some years later, Harold fell ill and died. There was a small funeral, and a few older winemakers came out to pay their respects.

There had been a problem, though, after Harold died. When people came up to Harold's house, they were confronted by his dog – that old stray he had picked up some years back. He'd even built that odd-looking house for the dog, right there on the front porch.

The dog wouldn't let anyone up the stairs when they approached. It just stood there on the front porch, tail sharp in the air, the fur standing up on its back, its feet widely planted, and it wailed in a low lamenting rhythm.

COLE DANEHOWER IS A JAMES BEARD FOUNDATION JOURNALISM AWARD-WINNING WINE WRITER AND AUTHOR OF THE BOOK *ESSENTIAL WINES AND WINERIES OF THE PACIFIC NORTHWEST* (TIMBER PRESS) WHO HAS REPORTED ON THE NORTHWEST WINE SCENE SINCE 1998. HE WRITES FOR A VARIETY OF PUBLICATIONS AND CURRENTLY PUBLISHES REGIONAL WINE JOURNALISM AT ESSENTIALNORTHWESTWINES.COM. HE IS OWNED BY MONTY, AN EXCEPTIONALLY INTELLIGENT AND RAMBUNCTIOUS CHOW/GOLDEN RETRIEVER MIX.
THIS STORY HAS BEEN REPRINTED FROM *WINE DOGS USA*, PUBLISHED 2006.

LEO

OWNER: ARIANA PEJU
FAVORITE FOOD: CHICKEN
PET PEEVE: WAKING UP AT 6AM
KNOWN ACCOMPLICE: HIS SISTER MINI
NAUGHTIEST DEED: PICKING ON BIG DOGS
FAVORITE PASTIME: GUARDING PEJU FROM WELCOMED GUESTS
OBSESSION: HEAD-TO-BEAK FIGHTING WITH THE CHICKEN THROUGH THE FENCE

MINI

PET PEEVE: GROOMING DAY
FAVORITE TOY: HER BLANKET
OWNER: HERTA BEHESNKY PEJU
KNOWN ACCOMPLICE: HER BROTHER LEO
OBSESSION: STALKING AND CHASING THE BARN CAT
NAUGHTIEST DEED: JUMPING ON THE TABLE FOR FOOD WHEN NO ONE IS AROUND
FAVORITE PASTIME: RUNNING LAPS IN THE ROSE GARDEN AFTER DINNER WITH LEO

SOPHIE

OWNER: SANDRA ROBERTS
PET PEEVE: BEING BRUSHED
FAVORITE TOY: PURPLE ELEPHANT
NAUGHTIEST DEED: WEEDING IN THE GARDEN
FAVORITE PASTIMES: MEETING NEW DOGS AT ALSTON DOG PARK AND GETTING A GOOD BELLY RUB
FAVORITE FOODS: PEANUT BUTTER AND MARROW BONES

PATRON

FAVORITE FOOD: CHICKEN
FAVORITE TOY: HIS BABY BONE
OWNERS: CHRIS AND LINDA BEHR
PET PEEVE: BEING WITHOUT A STICK OR BONE
FAVORITE PASTIME: ENTERTAINING VISITORS
OBSESSION: HAVING SOMETHING IN HIS MOUTH AT ALL TIMES
KNOWN ACCOMPLICES: QUITO THE ALPACA AND COW #5222

RUBY

FAVORITE TOY: FRISBEES
OWNERS: CHRIS AND LINDA BEHR
OBSESSIONS: ANGUS COWS AND STARING YOU IN THE EYE WITH HER PAW IN YOUR HAND
PET PEEVE: NOT GETTING HER FIVE-MILE RUN EACH DAY
FAVORITE PASTIMES: PLAYING FRISBEE AND HERDING SHEEP
NAUGHTIEST DEED: STEALING AND BURYING PATRON'S BONES

ABI

OBSESSION: RUNNING
FAVORITE TOY: WALNUTS
OWNER: ANDREW HOXSEY
FAVORITE FOOD: PHEASANT NECKS
NAUGHTIEST DEED: CHASING RABBITS
FAVORITE PASTIME: UPLAND BIRD HUNTING

ROGAN

OWNER: KENDALL HOXSEY
FAVORITE TOY: PHEASANT CHEW TOY
PET PEEVES: SQUIRRELS AND PEOPLE IGNORING HIM
NAUGHTIEST DEED: ESCAPING FROM THE BACKYARD AND MAKING PEOPLE CHASE HIM THROUGH THE VINEYARDS
FAVORITE PASTIME: TAKING WALKS THROUGH THE VINEYARDS
OBSESSIONS: FOLLOWING KENDALL EVERYWHERE AND CHEWING CORKS
FAVORITE FOOD: GRILLED SALMON COOKED ON WINE BARREL OAK CHIPS

WOLF

OBSESSION: THE CAT
OWNER: MICHAEL BEAULAC
FAVORITE TOY: RUBBER KONG
FAVORITE FOOD: ANYTHING GRILLED
KNOWN ACCOMPLICE: THE CAT, "GOOD FORTUNE"
FAVORITE PASTIME: HANGIN' WITH THE FAMILY
PET PEEVE: NOT BEING ABLE TO SLEEP ON THE COUCH

ROYAL

OWNERS: AMES AND KATE MORISON
NAUGHTIEST DEED: MAKING OFF WITH A SAUSAGE AT THE LOCAL SLOW FOOD PICNIC
OBSESSION: MAINTAINING ALPHA STATUS
FAVORITE TOY: HER BED, AFTER A LONG DAY AT WORK
FAVORITE PASTIME: LEADING VISITORS ON A VINEYARD TOUR
FAVORITE FOOD: ANYTHING THE VINEYARD CREW SHARES AT LUNCHTIME

BELLA

PET PEEVE: LONG CAR RIDES
OWNERS: CHRIS AND BRADLEY JAMES
OBSESSION: FORMERLY OBSESSED WITH BARKING BUT NOW QUIET AS A LAMB
NAUGHTIEST DEED: GETTING MUDDY (ONCE)
FAVORITE PASTIME: SPA DAY AT THE DOG GROOMERS
FAVORITE TOY: PREFERS RIBBONS AND BOWS TO TOYS

LOLA

OWNERS: KIM AND GARY MILLER
FAVORITE PASTIME: RIDING SHOTGUN
KNOWN ACCOMPLICES: BUDDY AND OTIS
FAVORITE FOOD: BURGERS OFF THE GRILL
NAUGHTIEST DEED: BEING AN ESCAPE ARTIST
PET PEEVE: INFREQUENT FAN CLUB MEMBERS
FAVORITE TOY: ANY BALL... ANY TIME... ANYWHERE!

ELE

PET PEEVE: KIDS GETTING INTO HER CRATE
FAVORITE TOY: OLD DUCK DECOY (MISSING ITS HEAD)
NAUGHTIEST DEED: JUMPING INTO THE BATHTUB WITH THE KIDS AND THEN RUNNING AROUND THE HOUSE
FAVORITE FOOD: BLUE BUFFALO FREEDOM (GRAIN FREE)
OWNERS: JEFF, REBECCA, ALEXIS, TRISTAN AND PEYTON HILL
OBSESSION: CARRYING SHOES IN HER MOUTH AND JUMPING INTO WATER

LABRADOR, 10 MONTHS | **HILL WINE COMPANY** ST. HELENA, CA

GINGER

OWNER: RYAN MESSINA
FAVORITE TOY: ALLIGATOR
FAVORITE FOOD: DOG TREATS
PET PEEVE: RIDING IN THE CAR
OBSESSION: LICKING HER RIGHT PAW
KNOWN ACCOMPLICES: CODY, TIMON AND CRUSH
FAVORITE PASTIME: CHASING RABBITS AND GOPHERS
NAUGHTIEST DEED: PICKING ON YORKSHIRE TERRIERS

LESKO

OBSESSION: TOYS
OWNER: KELLY FLEMING
FAVORITE FOODS: PROTEIN AND FRESH BREAD
FAVORITE TOY: ANYTHING THAT FITS INTO HIS MOUTH
PET PEEVE: SALLY BARKING NON-STOP WHILE HERDING TOYS
FAVORITE PASTIME: CHASING SALLY THROUGH THE VINEYARD
NAUGHTIEST DEED: SNEAKING FOOD OFF KITCHEN COUNTERS AT HOME

SALLY

OWNER: KELLY FLEMING
OBSESSION: TAUNTING LESKO
FAVORITE TOYS: VINEYARD ROCKS
FAVORITE PASTIME: HERDING BOCCE BALLS
FAVORITE FOOD: BBQ CRISPY-SKINNED CHICKEN
NAUGHTIEST DEED: UNSUCCESSFULLY HERDING THE CATS
PET PEEVE: LESKO COLLECTING AND NOT SHARING HER TOYS

IRIE

NAUGHTIEST DEED: CHEWING HOLES IN MEGAN'S BATHROBE
FAVORITE TOY: BARREL BUNGS
PET PEEVE: BEING LEFT ALONE
OWNERS: JUSTIN AND MEGAN MURPHY
OBSESSION: BEING RIGHT NEXT TO JUSTIN
FAVORITE PASTIMES: GREETING PEOPLE WITH A SMILE AND SUPERVISING THE WINERY CREW

BLEECKER

NAUGHTIEST DEED: EATING YUCKY STUFF OUT OF GARBAGE
FAVORITE FOOD: ANYTHING HE CAN STEAL OFF THE COUNTER
FAVORITE TOY: ANY TYPE OF BALL
OWNERS: JASON AND JENNIFER SMITH
FAVORITE PASTIME: PLAYING IN THE FOUNTAIN

AERO

FAVORITE PASTIME: RIDING ANYWHERE WITH JASON
NAUGHTIEST DEEDS: DIGGING HOLES AND HIDING IN THE CAR
OBSESSION: STEALING EVERYTHING
OWNERS: JASON AND JENNIFER SMITH
FAVORITE FOOD: BOLOGNA SANDWICHES

PATCH

PET PEEVE: BATHS
FAVORITE TOY: THE CAT
OWNERS: CHRIS AND BRENDA LYNCH
FAVORITE PASTIMES: BOASTING ABOUT HIS RACING DAYS AND SLEEPING
FAVORITE FOOD: ANYTHING FROM YOUR PLATE
NAUGHTIEST DEED: STEALING FOOD FROM THE PANTRY

GREYHOUND, 13 | **MUTT LYNCH WINERY** WINDSOR, CA

“Happiness is a warm puppy.”

CHARLES M. SCHULZ

YOU AIN'T NOTHIN' BUT A WINE DOG
(BEEN SNOOPIN' ROUND MY CELLAR DOOR...)

by Craig McGill and Susan Elliott

EVERY GREAT WINE-MAKER has a faithful dish-licker. Whether it's in the winery, the tasting room or just hangin' around the vineyard, they go together like burgers and fries, hot dogs and ketchup or pinot noir and duck.

In our books, we try to capture the rich personalities of the winery dog and to celebrate the humor, playfulness, trust and affection of these wonderful creatures. The dogs may be different shapes and sizes but each portrait evokes the deep love and the enduring pleasure that these pooches bring to our lives.

In this Californian edition, we draw special attention to the canines from the Golden State's wineries. Like the estates themselves, some wine dogs are swanky and spectacular; some are rustic and laid-back and some are high profile and high flyers. But they are all quintessentially 'Californian' (which is often said to be a state of mind after all).

Our travels for this book led us to Tara Bella Winery in Sonoma where we met Presley and Thornton *(page 41)*. These two hound dogs were named as a tribute to 'The King of Rock n' Roll', Elvis Presley, and the great blues singer, Big Mama Thornton, who first recorded the hit 'Hound Dog'. To top it off, these two Wine Dogs loved to belt out a tune!

When we arrived at the tasting room, we were greeted by the pair, wearing fezzes and ready to vogue for our camera. Talk about ready-made stars, these hounds must have read their own press releases. We can't remember laughing so much during a photo shoot and as a result have dined out on the story for months.

Another memorable photo-shoot was at Herman Story Winery in Paso Robles *(page 11)*. It's a cool urban winery in downtown Paso Robles that produces some of the best wines in California – balanced and lip-smackingly good. But it was their dogs that really got us in. Hank, a noble and masterful pointer, was a veritable canine ball-magnet and nothing could get past him as he raced and retrieved every tennis ball in sight.

That was until Abby, an Alapaha Bulldog cross, arrived at the winery. Being very low-to-the-ground, Abby would swoop with the deft skill of an eagle and retrieve the ball before Hank knew what day it was. She was good at retrieving, *very* good, but not so good at releasing... and so the process was repeated with a second ball. Same result. Now Abby had both balls in her mouth... and then a third. Well, we ran out of balls after that...

Looking back, it was also the people that made this book so enjoyable to publish. The times spent with Robert Mondavi and Fess Parker are memories we'll always cherish as well as the photoshoot with Mike Grgich and his loyal dog Posip – lots of fun that was taken to another level by their love of these four-legged creatures we call our best friends. Also a special mention to perhaps the greatest dog lover of them all, Robert Parker. Robert's dogs are part of their family and he is always keen to share what antics they've been up to.

We must admit, the dogs featured in our Wine Dogs books are not always as well trained or as good as they appear to be, but nevertheless, enjoy and let these dogs make your day.

PHOTOGRAPHY

Craig with Tule Bollibakka from Silver Oak Cellars, Oakville CA

SUSAN ELLIOTT

PUBLISHER, DESIGNER

Susan is a multi-skilled artist with a background in fine art, illustration and printmaking. After studying psychology, Sue changed to a career in art. She graduated from The City Art Institute in 1986, majoring in drawing, printmaking and painting.

After living abroad, Sue returned to Australia and exhibited her graphic art and screenprints extensively around Sydney, while also working in a number of small design studios. She has developed into an award-winning graphic designer with over 20 years of experience in the industry.

Sue joined McGill Design Group in 1999 as co-owner and Creative Director. She is also co-founder and principal of the Giant Dog publishing house, which is responsible for producing a number of best-selling books, including the *Wine Dogs* titles. She recently designed five *Wine Dogs* stamps for Australia Post.

Sue's knowledge of dogs is unparalleled, and in the past she has also found time to be a successful Siberian Husky breeder. Although currently dogless, Sue loves to spend time with the many wine dogs she meets from around the world as well as a feisty Green Severum named Ron.

CRAIG McGILL

PUBLISHER, PHOTOGRAPHER

Originally from Shepparton in Victoria, Australia, Craig is a self-taught designer and illustrator who started his own design business in Melbourne at 18 years of age. During that time he was appointed as a design consultant to The Reserve Bank of Australia.

His designs and illustrations have graced banknotes throughout the world, including the Australian bicentenary ten-dollar note. His work appears on the original Australian $100 note, Papua New Guinea Kina, Cook Islands Dollars and English Pound traveller's cheques. Craig was also involved in the design and illustration of many countries' security documents such as Passports, Bonds and Traveller's Cheques.

At the age of 23 he designed the entire series of the Cook Islands banknotes and it is believed that he was the world's youngest designer to design a country's complete currency. In 1991, Craig moved to Sydney where his illustrations were regularly commissioned by agencies and designers both in Australia and around the world.

He is now widely known as Australia's only freelance currency designer. Craig has also designed and illustrated nine stamps for Australia Post. Five of his *Wine Dogs* photos have also been used on stamps for Australia Post.

Craig has been Creative Director of his own agency, McGill Design Group, for over twenty-five years.

Having grown up with a succession of beagles and huskies, Craig is currently road-testing several hundred dog breeds from wineries around the world. www.realnasty.com.au

---

GIANT DOG PUBLISHING

Giant Dog is a niche independent publishing house specialising in producing benchmark quality design and art books. Recent publications include *Wine Cats*, *Wine Dogs USA 3*, *Wine Dogs Australia 3*, *Wine Dogs Italy*, *Wine Dogs New Zealand* and *Footy Dogs*. www.giantdog.com.au

McGILL DESIGN GROUP

McGill Design Group was formed in 1981 and specialises in providing a wide range of quality graphic design services. The studio has produced numerous fine wine labels and packaging as well as corporate identities, advertising, publications and television commercials. www.mcgilldesigngroup.com

WINERY and VINEYARD LISTINGS

Amapola Creek Winery by Richard Arrowood PAGE 125
392 London Way
Sonoma CA 95476
Ph: 707 938 3783
www.amapolacreek.com

Arista Winery PAGE 49
7015 Westside Road
Healdsburg CA 95448
Ph: 707 473 0606
www.aristawinery.com

August Briggs Winery PAGE 143
1307 B Lincoln Avenue
Calistoga CA 94515
Ph: 707 942 4912
www.augustbriggswinery.com

Balo Vineyards PAGE 46
9001 Highway 128
Philo CA 95466
Ph: 707 895 3655
www.balovineyards.com

Beckmen Vineyards
PAGES 140, 141
2670 Ontiveros Road
Los Olivos CA 93441
Ph: 805 688 8664
www.beckmenvineyards.com

Benziger Family Winery
PAGES 34, 35
1883 London Ranch Road
Glen Ellen CA 95442
Ph: 800 989 8890
www.benziger.com

Bonny Doon Vineyard
PAGES 126, 127
450 Highway 1
Davenport CA 95017
Ph: 888 819 6789
www.bonnydoonvineyard.com

Bouchaine Vineyards PAGE 53
1075 Buchli Station Road
Napa CA 94559
Ph: 707 252 9065
www.bouchaine.com

Boyd Family Vineyard PAGE 123
4042 Big Ranch Road
Napa CA 94558
Ph: 707 265 9485
www.boydwine.com

Brander Vineyard PAGE 122
2401 N Refugio Road
Los Olivos CA 93441
Ph: 805 688 2455
www.brander.com

Brecon Estate PAGE 83
7450 Vineyard Drive
Paso Robles CA 93446
Ph: 805 239 2200
www.breconestate.com

Bridlewood Estate Winery
PAGES 6, 66, 67
3555 Roblar Avenue
Santa Ynez CA 93460
Ph: 805 688 9000
www.bridlewoodwinery.com

Carmel Ridge Winery PAGE 64
Tasting room:
700 Cannery Row, Suite C
Monterey CA 93940
Ph: 831 324 0035
www.carmelridge.com

Carr Vineyards and Winery
PAGE 93
414 N Salsipuedes Street
Santa Barbara CA 93103
Ph: 805 965 7985
www.carrwinery.com

Chamisal Vineyards PAGE 65
7525 Orcutt Road
San Luis Obispo CA 93401
Ph: 805 541 9463
www.chamisalvineyards.com

Charles Krug Winery PAGE 48
2800 Main Street
St. Helena CA 94574
Ph: 800 237 0033
www.charleskrug.com

Cimarone Wines PAGE 59
2982 Grand Avenue
Los Olivos CA 93441
Ph: 805 688 8011
www.cimarone.com

CLARBEC Wines PAGE 117
19368 Orange Avenue
Sonoma CA 95476
Ph: 707 996 4012
www.clarbecwines.com

Clos du Val PAGES 32, 33
5330 Silverado Trail
Napa CA 94558
Ph: 707 261 5200
www.closduval.com

Clos La Chance Winery
PAGES 128, 129
1 Hummingbird Lane
San Martin CA 95046
Ph: 408 686 1050
www.clos.com

Cold Heaven Cellars PAGE 144
92 A 2nd Street
Buellton CA 93427
Ph: 805 686 1343
www.coldheavencellars.com

Cornell Winery and Tasting Room PAGE 131
29975 Mulholland Highway
Cornell CA 91301
Ph: 818 735 3542
www.cornellwinery.com

Crocker & Starr Winery PAGE 130
PO Box 987
St. Helena CA 94574
Ph: 707 967 9111
www.crockerstarr.com

D'Argenzio Winery PAGE 157
1301 Cleveland Avenue
Santa Rosa CA 95401
Ph: 707 546 2466
www.dargenziowine.com

Del Carlo Winery PAGES 133–135
4939 Dry Creek Road
Healdsburg CA 95448
Ph: 707 433 1036
www.delcarlowinery.com

Doce Robles PAGE 132
2023 Twelve Oaks Drive
Paso Robles CA 93446
Ph: 805 227 4766
www.docerobles.com

Donati Family Vineyard PAGE 54
2720 Oak View Road
Templeton CA 93465
Ph: 805 238 0676
www.donatiwine.com

Dunstan Wines, Durell Vineyard PAGES 146, 147
1945 Felder Road
Sonoma CA 95476
Ph: 707 933 3839
www.dunstanwines.com

Dutcher Crossing Winery
PAGE 23
8533 Dry Creek Road
Geyserville CA 95441
Ph: 707 431 2700
www.dutchercrossingwinery.com

Eberle Winery PAGE 55
3810 Highway 46 East
Paso Robles CA 93446
Ph: 805 238 9607
www.eberlewinery.com

El Molino Winery PAGE 149
3315 Saint Helena
Highway North
St. Helena CA 94574
Ph: 707 963 3632
www.elmolinowinery.com

Envolve Winery PAGE 148
27 E. Napa Street, Suite A
Sonoma CA 95476
Ph: 707 721 1979
www.envolvewinery.com

Ferrari-Carano Vineyards and Winery PAGE 155
8761 Dry Creek Road
Healdsburg CA 95448
Ph: 707 433 6700
www.ferrari-carano.com

Fess Parker Winery & Vineyard PAGE 159
6200 Foxen Canyon Road
Los Olivos CA 93441
Ph: 805 6881545
www.fessparkerwines.com

Firestone Vineyard PAGES 150, 151
5000 Zaca Station Road
Los Olivos CA 93441
Ph: 805 688 3940
www.firestonewine.com

Fortunati Vineyards PAGES 12, 13
986 Salvador Avenue
Napa CA 94558
Ph: 707 255 9300
www.fortunatiwines.com

Foxen PAGE 164
7600 Foxen Canyon Road
Santa Maria CA 93454
Ph: 805 937 4251
www.foxenvineyard.com

Freemark Abbey Winery PAGE 152
3022 St. Helena Highway North
St. Helena CA 95574
Ph: 707 302 3702
www.freemarkabbey.com

Frenchie Winery PAGE 61
849 Zinfandel Lane
St. Helena CA 94574
Ph: 707 963 3141
www.frenchiewinery.com

Frog's Leap PAGE 63
8815 Conn Creek Road
Rutherford CA 94573
Ph: 707 963 4704
www.frogsleap.com

Grgich Hills Estate PAGES 25–27
1829 St. Helena Highway
Rutherford CA 94573
Ph: 707 963 2784
www.grgich.com

Gundlach Bundschu Winery PAGE 62
2000 Denmark Street
Sonoma CA 95476
Ph: 707 939 3034
www.gunbun.com

Hall Wines PAGE 71
401 St. Helena Highway
St. Helena CA 94574
Ph: 707 967 2626
www.hallwines.com

Halter Ranch Vineyard PAGES 68–70
8910 Adelaida Road
Paso Robles CA 93446
Ph: 888 367 9977
www.halterranch.com

Hammersky Vineyards PAGE 60
7725 Vineyard Drive
Paso Robles CA 93446
Ph: 805 239 0930
www.hammersky.com

Harney Lane Winery PAGE 75
9010 E. Harney Lane
Lodi CA 95240
Ph: 209 365 1900
www.harneylane.com

Hawley Winery PAGE 74
6387 West Dry Creek Road
Healdsburg CA 95448
Ph: 707 473 9500
www.hawleywine.com

Hendry Ranch Winery PAGE 73
3104 Redwood Road
Napa CA 94558
Ph: 707 226 8320
www.hendrywines.com

Herb Lamb Vineyards PAGE 138
PO Box 225
St. Helena CA 94574
Ph: 707 967 9752
www.herblambvineyards.com,
www.twoolddogs.com

Herman Story Winery PAGE 11
1227 Paso Robles Street
Paso Robles CA 93446
Ph: 805 237 2400
www.hermanstorywines.com

Hill Family Estate PAGE 136
6512 Washington Street
Yountville CA 94599
Ph: 707 944 9580
www.hillfamilyestate.com

Hill Wine Company PAGE 183
1001 Silverado Trail South
St. Helena CA 94574
Ph: 707 963 7000
www.hillwinecompany.com

Hope & Grace Wines PAGE 72
6540 Washington Street
Yountville CA 94599
Ph: 707 944 2500
www.hopeandgracewines.com

Imagery Estate Winery PAGE 78
14335 Sonoma Highway
Glen Ellen CA 95442
Ph: 707 935 4515
www.imagerywinery.com

Jada Vineyard and Winery PAGE 184
5620 Vineyard Drive
Paso Robles CA 93446
Ph: 805 226 4200
www.jadavineyard.com

Jericho Canyon Vineyard PAGES 80, 81
3292 Old Toll Road
Calistoga CA 94515
Ph: 707 942 9665
www.jerichocanyonvineyard.com

Jessup Cellars PAGE 101
6740 Washington Street
Yountville CA 94599
Ph: 707 944 8523
www.jessupcellars.com

John Anthony Vineyards PAGE 82
1440 First Street, Napa CA 94559
Ph: 707 265 7711
www.johnanthonyvineyards.com

Jordan Vineyard & Winery PAGES 106, 107
1474 Alexander Valley Road
Healdsburg CA 95448
Ph: 707 431 5250
www.jordanwinery.com

Keenan Winery PAGES 84–86
3660 Spring Mountain Road
St. Helena CA 94574
Ph: 707 963 9177
www.keenanwinery.com

Keever Vineyards PAGE 16
PO Box 2906
Yountville CA 94599
Ph: 707 944 0910
www.keevervineyards.com

Kelham Vineyards PAGES 98, 99
360 Zinfandel Lane
St. Helena CA 94574
Ph: 707 963 2000
www.kelhamvineyards.com

Kelly Fleming Wines PAGE 185
2339 Pickett Road
Calistoga CA 94515
Ph: 707 942 6849
www.kellyflemingwines.com

Kendall-Jackson PAGES 114, 115
5007 Fulton Road
Fulton CA 95439
Ph: 866 287 9818
www.kj.com

Kinsella Estates PAGE 105
Healdsburg CA 95448
Ph: 855 707 8686
www.kinsellaestates.com

Klinker Brick Winery PAGE 102
15887 N Alpine Road
Lodi CA 95240
Ph: 209 333 1845
www.klinkerbrickwinery.com

Kosta Browne Winery
PAGES 90, 91
PO Box 1555
Sebastopol CA 95473
Ph: 707 823 7430
www.kostabrowne.com

Kunde Family Estate PAGE 92
9825 Sonoma Highway
Kenwood CA 95452
Ph: 707 833 5501
www.kunde.com

Larson Family Winery PAGE 95
23355 Millerick Road
Sonoma CA 95476
Ph: 707 938 3031
www.larsonfamilywinery.com

Lasseter Family Winery PAGE 120
1 Vintage Lane
Glen Ellen CA 95442
Ph: 707 933 2800
www.lasseterfamilywinery.com

Ledson Winery and Vineyards PAGES 96, 97
7335 Sonoma Highway
Kenwood CA 95409
Ph: 707 537 3823
www.ledson.com

Loma Prieta Winery PAGE 171
26985 Loma Prieta Way
Los Gatos CA 95033
Ph: 408 353 2950
www.lomaprietawinery.com

Lone Madrone PAGE 169
5800 Adelaida Road
Paso Robles CA 93446
Ph: 805 238 0845
www.lonemadrone.com

Ma(i)sonry Napa Valley PAGE 94
6711 Washington Street
Yountville CA 94599
Ph: 707 944 0889
www.maisonry.com

Mauritson Family Winery
PAGE 170
2859 Dry Creek Road
Healdsburg CA 95448
Ph: 707 431 0804
www.mauritsonwines.com

Medlock Ames PAGE 181
3487 Alexander Valley Road,
Healdsburg CA 95448
Ph: 707 431 8845
www.medlockames.com

Miller Wine Works PAGE 182
67 Main Street
Sutter Creek CA 95685
Ph: 209 267 5828
www.millerwineworks.com

Mutt Lynch Winery PAGE 187
9050 Windsor Road
Windsor CA 95492
Ph: 707 942 6180
www.muttlynchwinery.com

Napa Wine Company
PAGES 178, 179
7830 St. Helena Highway
Oakville CA 94562
Ph: 707 944 4481
www.napawineco.com

O'Brien Estate Winery PAGE 158
1200 Orchard Avenue
Napa CA 94558
Ph: 707 252 8463
www.obrienestate.com

Odette Estate Winery PAGE 176
5998 Silverado Trail
Napa CA 94558
Ph: 707 224 7533
www.odetteestate.com

Oso Libre Winery PAGE 177
7383 Vineyard Drive
Paso Robles CA 93446
Ph: 805 238 3378
www.osolibre.com

Pacific Star Winery PAGE 47
33000 N Highway 1
Fort Bragg CA 95437
Ph: 707 964 1155
www.pacificstarwinery.com

Papapietro Perry PAGE 172
4791 Dry Creek Road
Healdsburg CA 95448
Ph: 707 433 0422
www.papapietro-perry.com

Paraiso Vineyards PAGE 186
38060 Paraiso Springs Road
Soledad CA 93960
Ph: 831 678 0300
www.paraisovineyards.com

Peju Province Winery PAGE 175
8466 St. Helena Highway
Rutherford CA 94573
Ph: 707 963 3600
www.peju.com

Pine Ridge Vineyards PAGE 180
5901 Silverado Trail
Napa CA 94558
Ph: 800 486 0503
www.pineridgevineyards.com

Plumpjack Estate Winery
PAGE 79
620 Oakville Cross Road
Napa CA 94558
Ph: 707 945 1220
www.plumpjackwinery.com

Poalillo Vineyards PAGES 76, 77
7970 Vineyard Drive
Paso Robles CA 93446
Ph: 805 238 0621
www.poalillovineyards.com

Press Gang Cellars PAGE 142
Lompoc CA 93436
Ph: 805 291 3141
www.pressgangcellars.com

Provenance Vineyards PAGE 37
1695 St. Helena Highway
St. Helena CA 94574
Ph: 707 968 3633
www.provenancevineyards.com

Riverbench Vineyard and Winery PAGE 145
6020 Foxen Canyon Road
Santa Maria CA 93454
Ph: 805 937 8340
www.riverbench.com

ROAR Wines PAGE 15
32721 River Road
Soledad CA 93960
Ph: 831 675 1681
www.roarwines.com

Robert Mondavi Winery PAGE 89
Highway 29
Oakville CA 94562
Ph: 888 766 6328
www.robertmondavi.com

Rusack Vineyards PAGE 36
1819 Ballard Canyon Road
Solvang CA 93463
Ph: 805 688 1278
www.rusackvineyards.com

Saddleback Cellars PAGE 17
7802 Money Road
Oakville CA 94562
Ph: 707 944 1305
www.saddlebackcellars.com

Sanglier Cellars PAGE 38
132 Plaza Street
Healdsburg CA 95448
Ph: 707 433 6104
www.sangliercellars.com

Saucelito Canyon Vineyard
PAGE 39
3080 Biddle Ranch Road
San Luis Obispo CA 93401
Ph: 805 543 2111
www.SaucelitoCanyon.com

Sbragia Family Vineyards
PAGES 108, 109
9990 Dry Creek Road
Geyserville CA 95441
Ph: 707 473 2992
www.sbragia.com

Sequoia Grove Vineyards
PAGE 14
8338 St. Helena Highway
Napa CA 94558
Ph: 707 944 2945
www.sequoiagrove.com

Shafer Vineyards PAGE 31
6154 Silverado Trail
Napa CA 94558
Ph: 707 944 2877
www.shafervineyards.com

Silver Horse Winery
PAGES 160, 163
2995 Pleasant Road
San Miguel CA 93451
Ph: 805 467 9463
www.silverhorse.com

Silver Oak Cellars PAGES 28–30
915 Oakville Cross Road
Oakville CA 94562
Ph: 707 944 8808
www.silveroak.com

Silverado Vineyards PAGE 40
6121 Silverado Trail
Napa CA 94558
Ph: 707 257 1770
www.silveradovineyards.com

St. Francis Winery and Vineyards PAGES 50–52
500 Pythian Road
Santa Rosa CA 95409
Ph: 707 833 4666
www.stfranciswinery.com

St. Supéry Estate Vineyards and Winery PAGE 42, 43
8440 St. Helena Highway
Rutherford CA 94573
Ph: 707 963 4507
www.stsupery.com, www.facebook.com/GG.CCO

Stony Hill Vineyard PAGE 87
PO Box 308
St. Helena CA 94574
Ph: 707 963 2636
www.stonyhillvineyard.com

Storm Wines PAGE 22
5249 Foxen Canyon Road
Los Olivos CA 93441
Ph: 530 409 1875
www.stormwines.com

Tara Bella Winery PAGE 41
3701 Viking Road
Santa Rosa CA 95492
Ph: 707 544 9049
www.tarabellawinery.com

Thacher Winery PAGE 139
8355 Vineyard Drive
Paso Robles CA 93446
Ph: 805 237 0087
www.thacherwinery.com

Tin Barn Vineyards PAGE 153
21692 Eighth Street, East #340
Sonoma CA 95476
Ph: 707 938 5430
www.tinbarnvineyards.com

Tom Eddy Winery PAGE 166
3870 Highway 128
Calistoga CA 94515
Ph: 707 942 4267
www.tomeddywines.com

Trattore Estate Wines PAGE 19
7878 Dry Creek Road
Geyserville CA 95441
Ph: 707 431 7200
www.trattorefarms.com

Trefethen Family Vineyards
PAGE 100
1160 Oak Knoll Avenue
Napa CA 94558
Ph: 866 895 7696
www.trefethen.com

Trinitas Cellars PAGE 154
875 Bordeaux Way
Napa CA 94558
Ph: 888 983 8414
www.trinitascellars.com

Truchard Vineyards PAGE 124
3234 Old Sonoma Road
Napa CA 94559
Ph: 707 253 7153
www.truchardvineyards.com

Trujillo Wines PAGE 165
PO Box 866
Angwin CA 94508
Ph: 707 965 2943
www.trujillowines.com

Tudal Vineyards PAGE 18
1015 Big Tree Road
St. Helena CA 94574
Ph: 707 963 3947
www.tudalwinery.com

Turnbull Wine Cellars
PAGES 44, 45
8210 St. Helena Highway
Oakville CA 9456
Ph: 707 963 5839
www.turnbullwines.com

Tusk Estates PAGE 167
PO Box 126, Oakville CA 94562
www.tuskestates.com

Twisted Oak Winery PAGE 121
4280 Red Hill Road
Vallecito CA 95247
Ph: 209 736 9080
www.twistedoak.com

Vino Tabi Winery PAGE 168
334 Ingalls Street, C
Santa Cruz CA 95060
Ph: 831 426 1809
www.vino-tabi-wine.com

Vintner's Collective PAGE 24
1245 Main Street
Napa CA 94559
Ph: 707 255 7150
www.vcnv.com

Whitehall Lane Winery and Vineyards PAGES 110, 111
1563 St. Helena Highway
St. Helena CA 94574
Ph: 707 963 9454
www.whitehalllane.com

Wilderotter Vineyard PAGES 20, 21
19890 Shenandoah School Road
Plymouth CA 95669
Ph: 209 245 6016
www.wilderottervineyard.com

Wilson Winery PAGES 112, 113
1960 Dry Creek Road
Healdsburg CA 95448
Ph: 707 433 4355
www.wilsonwinery.com

WM Harrison Winery
PAGES 118, 119
1443 Silverado Trail S.
St. Helena CA 94574
Ph: 707 963 8310
www.whwines.com

WINE DOGS BREED INDEX

BODEGA SIX-YEAR-OLD LABRADOR AND **J.J.** TWELVE-YEAR-OLD LABRADOR, VINCENT ARROYO WINERY, CALISTOGA CA

TOOTSIE NINE-YEAR-OLD IRISH WOLFHOUND CROSS, MALOY O'NEILL VINEYARDS, PASO ROBLES CA

WINE DOGS CALIFORNIA
ISBN 978-1-921336-35-5

EDITING AND PROOFREADING BY VICKY FISHER

PRINTED BY 1010 PRINTING INTERNATIONAL LIMITED, CHINA.

PUBLISHED BY GIANT DOG, ABN 27 110 894 178.
PO BOX 964, ROZELLE NSW 2039 AUSTRALIA
TELEPHONE: (+612) 9555 4077
WWW.WINEDOGS.COM

FOR ORDERS: ORDERS@WINEDOGS.COM

OTHER TITLES BY CRAIG McGILL AND SUSAN ELLIOTT INCLUDE:
WINE DOGS: ORIGINAL EDITION – THE DOGS OF AUSTRALIAN WINERIES ISBN 0-9580856-1-7
WINE DOGS: DELUXE EDITION – THE DOGS OF AUSTRALASIAN WINERIES ISBN 0-9580856-2-5
FOOTY DOGS: THE DOGS OF AUSTRALIAN RULES FOOTBALL ISBN 0-9580856-3-3
WINE DOGS AUSTRALIA – MORE DOGS FROM AUSTRALIAN WINERIES ISBN 978-1-921336-02-7
WINE DOGS AUSTRALIA 2 – MORE DOGS FROM AUSTRALIAN WINERIES ISBN 978-1-921336-16-4
WINE DOGS AUSTRALIA 3 – MORE DOGS FROM AUSTRALIAN WINERIES ISBN 978-1-921336-28-7
WINE DOGS: USA EDITION – THE DOGS OF NORTH AMERICAN WINERIES ISBN 0-9580856-6-8
WINE DOGS USA 2 – MORE DOGS FROM NORTH AMERICAN WINERIES ISBN 978-1-921336-10-2
WINE DOGS USA 3 – MORE DOGS FROM NORTH AMERICAN WINERIES ISBN 978-1-921336-29-4
WINE DOGS ITALY – THE DOGS OF ITALIAN WINERIES ISBN 978-1-921336-11-9
WINE DOGS NEW ZEALAND – THE DOGS OF NEW ZEALAND WINERIES ISBN 978-1-921336-12-6
WINE CATS ISBN 978-1-921336-38-6

HEALTH WARNING: VETERINARY ASSOCIATIONS ADVISE THAT EATING GRAPES, SULTANAS OR RAISINS CAN MAKE A DOG EXTREMELY ILL AND COULD POSSIBLY RESULT IN FATAL KIDNEY FAILURE. IN THE INTERESTS OF CANINE HEALTH AND WELLBEING, DO NOT FEED YOUR DOG GRAPES OR ANY GRAPE BY-PRODUCT.